Perceiving
the Wheel of God

The Suffering Series

D1522924

Perceiving
the Wheel of God

The Suffering Series

Dr. Mark Hanby

Edited by David Singleton

Destiny Image Publishers
P.O. Box 310
Shippensburg, PA 17257

"Speaking to the Purposes
of God for this Generation"

ISBN 1-56043-109-1

For Worldwide Distribution
Printed in the U.S.A.

Destiny Image books are available through these fine distributors outside the United States:

Christian Growth, Inc.
Jalan Kilang-Timor, Singapore 0315

Successful Christian Living
Capetown, Rep. of South Africa

Lifestream
Nottingham, England

Vision Resources
Ponsonby, Auckland, New Zealand

Rhema Ministries Trading
Randburg, South Africa

WA Buchanan Company
Geebung, Queensland, Australia

Salvation Book Centre
Petaling, Jaya, Malaysia

Word Alive
Niverville, Manitoba, Canada

Contents

Chapter Outline

In Chapter 1, we discover that the process of becoming a vessel for God is akin to the process of molding a clay vessel on a potter's wheel. As we are fashioned and reshaped through spinning disorientation, we can choose to stay on the wheel and be molded into God's workmanship, or we can eject ourselves from the process and refuse the purpose and peace of God.

Chapters 2 and 3 reveal to us that it is God who sends and allows trials of fire to clarify and temper us to grow in strength and purity. The baptism of fire spoken of by John the Baptist and the Lord Jesus was not referring to tingling excitement or bells of joy. Rather, the fire of God burns away false motive and desire, separating bad from good and excellent from good; just as winnowing and fire separate the true grain from chaff. Suffering with Christ and for Christ is not a choice, but a necessity to form powerful Christian character and biblical sanctification.

Our fourth chapter deals with the process of anointing. A life that is truly anointed of God will be a life of sacrifice. As the olive oil is released only through the pressure of the olive press, the anointing that God places within is drawn out through the trials of our faith. And as the anointing oil was mixed with various substances, it is the combination of both our bitter and sweet experiences that join together in a divine blending of godly endowment. There is also a geometry of the cross, representing the vertical and the horizontal of our lives. We offer both sacrifices to God and in doing so give offense to our fellow man.

In Chapter 5 we see that our experiences of joy and suffering are not haphazard events of a disorderly universe. Instead there is a divine synchronization and order in our triumphs and our trials. There is a pattern in our sufferings which serves the purpose of God. And when we understand the purpose of God in our breakings we have faith for the process.

Suffering is inevitable. We will all suffer in this life; generally as a human being living in a fallen world and particularly as we follow Christ in His sufferings. We must, however, learn to suffer successfully, which is the subject of our sixth chapter. When we truly know that God is the Potter and we are the clay, that the pressure of molding and the heat of the fire perform divine service and lead to His purpose and glory, then we will triumph over whatever becomes or falls to us.

In our final chapter we learn that the call of God upon a life brings with it a crucible and persecution that burns away the dross and serves to purify our hearts. It is in the hand of one who has suffered that the rod of leadership is held in firm compassion. To this end, we must perceive the wheel of God.

Editor's Note: This book has been developed from recordings of Dr. Hanby's messages on this subject over the last decade. We have carefully edited the material and included Scripture references to help further your personal study of this vital subject.

Chapter 1

Perceiving the Wheel of God
The Potter's Wheel

The word which came to Jeremiah from the Lord, saying,

Arise, and go down to the potter's house, and there I will cause thee to hear My words.

Then I went down to the potter's house, and, behold, he wrought a work on the wheels.

And the vessel that he made of clay was marred in the hand of the potter: so he made it again another vessel, as seemed good to the potter to make it.

Then the word of the Lord came to me, saying,

O house of Israel, cannot I do with you as this potter? saith the Lord. Behold, as the clay is in the potter's hand, so are ye in Mine hand, O house of Israel.

Jeremiah 18:1-6

I was praying early in the morning in keeping with my burden for the Church throughout the world. I have made it my life's work to pray this prayer: "God, I want to do Your will!"

The Lord spoke to my mind clearly. It was as though someone had shaken me, turned me around, and spoken to me. "You will never know My will until you first perceive the wheel of God."

I stopped and said, "I don't know what You mean."

For a long time, I pondered the words, "perceiving the wheel of God." *I will never know the will of God until I first perceive the wheel of God.*

The prayer, "O God, I want to do Your will,"[1] is uttered daily throughout the world. Every minister profusely prays it. Musicians who are in tune with spiritual things will not enter into service without saying it. However, you can never know the will of God until you perceive His wheel.

One of the first ingenious acts of man was the invention of the wheel; it was one of the first production tools. The first wheel ever created was the potter's wheel. You cannot have anything in industry without the wheel, the thing that goes around.

Everything in life is a cycle. The life cycle of humanity is part of the life cycle of other life forms. The life cycle of a tree is a part of the life cycle of other things.

The planetary system is a cycle. The farthest star and the nearest star are cycles. They all go around. The earth rotates around the sun. The moon rotates around the earth. Everything in the solar system rotates around something else. God's creation is built on a wheel.[2]

Everything that is a part of God's Kingdom is built on a wheel. If you can't perceive that, God will never use you in His will. You have to know you are on the wheel. You're not just having trouble. Someone hasn't just singled you out to talk bad about you. The Potter has His fingers in your spirit.

Deliverance from darkness into light[3] was a milestone in our lives. However, although the new birth alone did not perfect us, we feel there is nothing more for us to gain spiritually than what we received in that experience. Being repentant, forgiven, baptized, filled, and thrilled is not the end of all spiritual things. Deliverance is not the end, but the beginning. The new birth is not perfection, but an infantile beginning of life.

> *Therefore leaving the principles of the doctrine of Christ, let us go on unto perfection; not laying again the foundation of repentance from dead works, and of faith toward God,*
>
> *Of the doctrine of baptisms, and of laying on of hands, and of resurrection of the dead, and of eternal judgment.*
>
> Hebrews 6:1-2

We must go on to perfection after we have experienced these things. It will be a glorious day when the Church discovers this. We receive glorious restoration because we have a solid foundation. Now we can build on it.[4] We start with foundational truth, but we must build the sidewalls, the superstructure, and the roof on that foundation. After that, we lay the carpet and other things which are part of the building. The building isn't perfected just because we lay the foundation. There's still building to be done in us after we receive the new birth.[5]

If we do not perceive the wheel of God, we will become confused, hanging on to that initial experience. We will be so busy guarding it that we cannot reach the lost because we are unable to love others.

People who are able to proceed from that spiritual beginning have a basis for everything they do. They pray, "Lord, I want Your will in my life." Prayer—not money or status—is the basis for every decision that is made in their lives.[6] God is the basis for everything they do. Everything in the Christian life revolves around the will of God.

God answers that prayer when it is earnestly asked.[7] We pray against ourselves when we pray to know the will of God. He hears our prayer for the will of God and throws us right in the middle of the wheel. The wheel of God is the chastening of the Lord. He puts His hands on us and begins a work in our lives. When you are on the Potter's wheel, you have to yield to the motion of the Potter as He puts pressure in some areas.[8] If you do not endure chastening, you are an illegitimate child, a child who is not recognized by his father.

And ye have forgotten the exhortation which speaketh unto you as unto children, My son, despise not thou the chastening of the Lord, nor faint when thou art rebuked of Him:

For whom the Lord loveth He chasteneth, and scourgeth every son whom He receiveth.

If ye endure chastening, God dealeth with you as with sons; for what son is he whom the father chasteneth not?

But if ye be without chastisement, whereof all are partakers, then are ye bastards, and not sons.

Furthermore we have had fathers of our flesh which corrected us, and we gave them reverence: shall we not much rather be in subjection unto the Father of spirits, and live?

For they verily for a few days chastened us after their own pleasure; but He for our profit, that we might be partakers of His holiness.

Now no chastening for the present seemeth to be joyous, but grievous: nevertheless afterward it yieldeth the peaceable fruit of righteousness unto them which are exercised thereby.

Hebrews 12:5-11

He chastens every son He receives. Some people God calls are never used in His service. They are idle preachers in the field. They make shadows that never move. They are not useful harvesters. They may have prayed for the will of God, but they failed to perceive His wheel. You will never do anything for God until He chastens you.

If you know that, faith tells you that everything is all right. It doesn't matter how many doctors are bent over you if you know you're on the wheel.[9] Even if they tell you that you will die, knowing that you are on the wheel will sustain you.[10]

No matter how many foes are waiting for you, a thousand shall fall at your right hand.[11] You are under the shadow of the Almighty.[12] He is the Potter and you are on His wheel.[13] You must perceive that. Otherwise, everything God does in your life to create trust, love, and faith becomes anger, bitterness, disappointment, doubt, and fear. All you can do is go back to the foundation of truth, and say, "Come get me, Jesus."

When we start going around and around, we usually pray the other direction. "Oh, God, please come get me out of this!" You have already prayed for the will of God. If you don't perceive the wheel, one prayer cancels out another. Which prayer do you want God to hear? You pray for the will of God, He puts you on the wheel, and you pray, "Get me off this wheel!"

"Oh, God, use me. I want to be a mighty missionary." God puts you on the wheel, and you say, "Oh, God, I didn't expect this!" You didn't perceive the wheel.

You pray, "Oh, Lord! I will fast and pray until my whole family gets saved!" A few days later, you are eating crackers and milk and have given up on everything.

Oh that Thou wouldest rend the heavens, that Thou wouldest come down, that the mountains might flow down at Thy presence,

As when the melting fire burneth, the fire causeth the waters to boil, to make Thy name known to Thine adversaries, that the nations may tremble at Thy presence!

When Thou didst terrible things which we looked not for, Thou camest down, the mountains flowed down at Thy presence.

For since the beginning of the world men have not heard, nor perceived by the ear, neither hath the eye seen, O God, beside Thee, what He hath prepared for him that waiteth for Him.

Thou meetest him that rejoiceth and worketh righteousness, those that remember Thee in Thy ways: behold, Thou art wroth; for we have sinned: in those is continuance, and we shall be saved.

But we are all as an unclean thing, and all our righteousnesses are as filthy rags; and we all do fade as a leaf; and our iniquities, like the wind, have taken us away.

And there is none that calleth upon Thy name, that stirreth up himself to take hold of Thee: for Thou hast hid Thy face from us, and hast consumed us, because of our iniquities.

But now, O Lord, Thou art our father; we are the clay, and Thou our potter; and we all are the work of Thy hand.

Isaiah 64:1-8

This chapter begins with the prophet saying, "God, why don't You come down here and do something?" The prophet was praying that the mountains would shake and burn, and the fires would boil the water. When it happened, it happened in an unexpected way. "We didn't expect this!" Isaiah was not perceiving the wheel. God did what Isaiah prayed, but Isaiah didn't expect it like that.

This Scripture is not talking about streets of gold.[14] God has prepared something for you right now that you cannot see because you fail to perceive the wheel.

After God created the worlds (there are 150 billion stars in Andromeda in our galaxy, and there are over 150 billion galaxies larger than our own), innumerable companies of angels thought, "We didn't expect this. We thought we would be all the creation."[15]

God spotlighted one little planet called Earth and planted a garden.[16] God made many little creatures that had nothing to do with angelic force. He scraped a little clay together and formed the measure of Himself in dirt.[17] God stretched Himself over that form while the angels watched. He breathed His breath, the breath of life, into that dirt. Those angels said, "We didn't expect that."

I've known men who said they were going on a 30-day fast with nothing but water. Two weeks later, they were drinking juice and eating fruit. Three weeks later, they were eating steak, trying to regain their composure and strength. They lost their jobs, they made their wives mad, and their kids were sick. They said, "Every time I try to draw near to God, I have trouble you can't believe. Every time I try to get close to God it just seems like everything goes wrong." God answered their prayer and put them on the wheel. They didn't perceive what God did.

My brethren, count it all joy when ye fall into divers temptations,

Knowing this, that the trying of your faith worketh patience.

James 1:2-3

Wherein ye greatly rejoice, though now for a season, if need be, ye are in heaviness through manifold temptations:

That the trial of your faith, being much more precious than of gold that perisheth, though it be tried with fire, might be found unto praise and honour and glory at the appearing of Jesus Christ.

1 Peter 1:6-7

You can rejoice in tribulation only if you perceive the wheel of God. You must know God is trying you and putting pressure on you to shape you. You're enduring this trial so you can help others in similar predicaments.[18] When He has to push a little harder like a doctor setting a bone, it hurts. You don't want Him to do that anymore.

God loves us so much He wants us to become the quality that He knows we can be.[19] Only He knows what we can be if we wait for Him on the wheel. The Potter already has a vision of the vessel in His mind. He already knows what the finished product will be. It may only be lumpy, old clay, but the Potter has a peculiar purpose for this vessel. You may just be a blob now, but the Potter already sees you as holding the precious wine for a king. You may hold the oil for the fire or the spark for revival. You may be the vessel that will carry the fire from the valley to Moriah where a precious sacrifice may foreshadow Christ. First, though, the hands of the Potter must make you on the wheel.

God will meet the man who rejoices anyway. That man will read the Bible anyway. It doesn't matter what people say about him or how he feels. He loves the Lord anyway. Even if he loses jobs every day, he will still be in the house of the Lord. He will not become angry at the preacher or disquieted with the brethren. He knows what is happening to him. God will use him. He stays on the wheel with rejoicing and righteous works.

God will not put more on you than you are able to bear.[20] You lose your trust if you become angry and say that God is dead. You do not perceive the wheel of God if you think the Lord has forsaken you. It is easy to say, "You have sinned, and God hates you." You may think that God doesn't love you because of something you have done. You need to stop thinking that way.

Most people spend more time praying for forgiveness than for anything else. Every time you get in trouble, you pray, "Oh God, forgive me. I haven't been praying like I should."

Then one of the twelve, called Judas Iscariot, went unto the chief priests,

And said unto them, What will ye give me, and I will deliver Him unto you? And they covenanted with him for thirty pieces of silver.

And from that time he sought opportunity to betray Him.

Matthew 26:14-16

Judas may have been envious because Jesus always called Peter, James, and John to be alone with Him.[21] That may have been what made him think more about the money than the Man. When he was left out of the inner circle, he may have reasoned in his own heart, *Why don't I ever get to play in the orchestra?* or, *Why don't I ever get to preach?* especially since he was so much smarter and more talented than these fishermen. His mind began conceiving other things, and he created a plot to make money while waiting for a praying Master.[22]

Judas did not think they could take Jesus. He had escaped out of their hands before when they had tried to take Him.[23] How could they take Jesus? He was much too powerful for them. Judas did not expect that they could crucify Jesus.

And while He yet spake, lo, Judas, one of the twelve, came, and with him a great multitude with swords and staves, from the chief priests and elders of the people.

Now he that betrayed Him gave them a sign, saying, Whomsoever I shall kiss, that same is He: hold Him fast.

And forthwith he came to Jesus, and said, Hail, master; and kissed Him.

And Jesus said unto him, Friend, wherefore art thou come? Then came they, and laid hands on Jesus, and took Him.

Matthew 26:47-50

Judas kissed the gate of Heaven and went to hell. When Judas saw that Jesus was condemned, he repented himself and brought the 30 pieces of silver back to the temple.

Then Judas, which had betrayed Him, when he saw that He was condemned, repented himself, and brought again the thirty pieces of silver to the chief priests and elders,

Saying, I have sinned in that I have betrayed the innocent blood. And they said, What is that to us? see thou to that.

And he cast down the pieces of silver in the temple, and departed, and went and hanged himself.

And the chief priests took the silver pieces, and said, It is not lawful for to put them into the treasury, because it is the price of blood.

And they took counsel, and bought with them the potter's field, to bury strangers in.

Wherefore that field was called, The field of blood, unto this day.

Matthew 27:3-8

Judas went back to the church. Many people cast their lots to die, not in the beer joints or on a smoky job, but in the church. Jealousy treats you worst of all.[24] Bitterness creeps in because you failed to perceive the wheel of God and are unwilling to take your just due under the hand of the Potter.[25]

Sometimes you choose to be bitter and angry rather than trusting, precious, and sweet. Sometimes you choose gossip rather than faith and prayer. That is how the die is cast in the church.

Jeremiah saw more than just the potter. He saw the field full of potsherds left from clay vessels that would not yield to the potter's hand to mold them. They became too hard, refused the pressure, and would not stay on the wheel. The potter had no choice but to cast them away. Sometimes a potter's field is piled six or eight feet deep with potsherds, pieces of clay that refused to be made. The potter put them on a wheel and they refused to be made. There is no choice but to cast them out.

When Jeremiah went down to the potter's house according to the word of the Lord, he saw more than the potter's wheel. He saw what happens to those who do not stay on it. While he was at the potter's house, he *might* have bought the potter out.

"The Lord told me to come down here and I would learn some lessons. Would you sell this place?"

"Well, I don't know if I could sell my house," replied the potter, "but I would sell that field for thirty pieces of silver."

No, probably not. Jeremiah simply bought the lesson of the potter's wheel and learned to weep. Judas would later buy the potter's field, and die.

Everything the prophet did reflected things that would come to pass.[26]

The potter's field is all around our churches, littered with the broken bodies of those who refused to be made. Don't become weary of the spinning of the wheel. You may find yourself buried in the field of strangers.

We pray for revival and the Church prays against it. They don't want revival. They don't want prayer meetings because people start seeing visions, angels, and spiritual things.[27] So they shut them down. They don't want the gifts of the Spirit,[28] because people prophesy out of their own hearts and might say anything. Everything that would point the way to revival is rejected by the Church.

When the Church prays for revival, God puts it on the wheel. Then the Church refuses to be made. They don't want to do the things that God directs because of problems involved. It leaves a field of broken pottery. They prayed for the will of God against themselves, then begged to be removed from the wheel. No wonder there is such confusion in the Church.[29]

Endnotes—Chapter 1

1. Hebrews 10:7
2. Isaiah 40:22
3. Ephesians 5:8; 1 Peter 2:9
4. 1 Corinthians 3:12
5. John 3:3,5
6. James 4:13-16
7. 1 Peter 1:17
8. Romans 9:20-23; Isaiah 29:16
9. 1 John 5:4
10. 1 John 3:19-21
11. Psalm 91:7
12. Psalm 91:1
13. Isaiah 64:8
14. Revelation 21:21
15. Nehemiah 9:6
16. Ezekiel 28:13; Genesis 2:8
17. Genesis 2:7
18. Hebrews 5:2
19. Ephesians 4:13
20. 1 Corinthians 10:13
21. Matthew 17:1; Mark 5:37, et al.
22. John 12:4-6
23. Luke 4:30; John 8:59; 10:39
24. Song of Solomon 8:6
25. Matthew 20:7

26. Ezekiel 12:6,11
27. Acts 23:6-10
28. 1 Corinthians 12:8-10
29. Acts 19:29

Chapter 2

The Fire
I Have Created the Smith

Sing, O barren, thou that didst not bear; break forth into singing, and cry aloud, thou that didst not travail with child: for more are the children of the desolate than the children of the married wife, saith the Lord.

Enlarge the place of thy tent, and let them stretch forth the curtains of thine habitations: spare not, lengthen thy cords, and strengthen thy stakes;

For thou shalt break forth on the right hand and on the left; and thy seed shall inherit the Gentiles, and make the desolate cities to be inhabited.

Isaiah 54:1-3

O thou afflicted, tossed with tempest, and not comforted, behold, I will lay thy stones with fair colours, and lay thy foundations with sapphires.

And I will make thy windows of agates, and thy gates of carbuncles, and all thy borders of pleasant stones.

Isaiah 54:11-12

Sometimes you think that everything in the world has come against you. You can't understand why God would let this happen to you. Why didn't God rescue you before you fell into this much trouble? It is embarrassing for your pain to become so obvious to everyone.

God lays foundations with sapphires and precious stones of different colors.[1] Blasts of fire create those things. God is not satisfied with a foundation of mud or sandstone.

What you see, what you hear, what you say, and what you stand on must be tempered by fire.[2] He won't put anybody in the field that hasn't been to boot camp. The discipline of fire comes upon everyone in the field.

> *In righteousness shalt thou be established: thou shalt be far from oppression; for thou shalt not fear: and from terror; for it shall not come near thee.*
>
> *Behold, they shall surely gather together, but not by Me: whosoever shall gather together against thee shall fall for thy sake.*
>
> *Behold, I have created the smith that bloweth the coals in the fire, and that bringeth forth an instrument for his work; and I have created the waster to destroy.*
>
> *No weapon that is formed against thee shall prosper; and every tongue that shall rise against thee in judgment thou shalt condemn. This is the heritage of the servants of the Lord, and their righteousness is of Me, saith the Lord.*

Isaiah 54:14-17

You won't be oppressed because you won't fear.[3] You may get in trouble and have to endure affliction, but it won't oppress, suppress, depress, or compress you. You are not afraid to go through fire.[4]

Fire makes us look and feel uncomfortable. We don't like fire. We try to hide behind the masks we wear. God will remove the masks. God wants people to come clean with

Him. He wants people who will say to the accuser, "This is what I am, whether you like it or not." If you can say that, the devil can't hurt you. If you come clean with God, you will not fear the devil. He can't blow your cover if you don't have one. The fire burns it away.

No weapon formed against you can prosper.[5] God is the one who creates the smith that blows the coals.[6] You thought the devil was the one who was messing things up in your life, but God was the One supervising it all.[7]

When I was a boy, I walked past the blacksmith's shop every day on my way home from school. Joe, the blacksmith, was a big man who worked on the old farm tools. In the springtime when it was warm, we weren't in a big hurry to get home, so we would watch him work. He always opened up his shop to keep the circulation going because of the heat. He was sweating and his arm, black from his work, would smear his face.

From time to time, he would throw things in the big furnace in the middle of the shop. It was a big fire. The top of it was red hot. He used tongs to put things in the furnace, and he pumped the bellows with a foot pedal. "Joe, what are you doing?" I asked.

"I'm blowing the coals," he said.

"Why are you blowing the coals?" I asked.

"I'm blowing the coals to make the fire hotter. If I don't get it hot enough, I can't make this thing fit right."

"What good does it do to blow the coals?" I asked again.

"When I push on this pedal, it has a ballast that gathers air together and blows oxygen in the bottom of the furnace," he said. "That makes the coals hotter."

He reached in the fire with tongs, pulled that thing out, and laid it on the anvil. Then he hit it with the hammer.

He beat on that thing so hard and so long that I thought, *This man is a monster. He's a destructive animal. He's destroying everything he touches.*

God is the One who controls the bellows. Don't think all your problems come from the devil who is running loose doing everything he can to you. God said, "I am the One who created the smith who blows the coals."[8]

There hath no temptation taken you but such as is common to man: but God is faithful, who will not suffer you to be tempted above that ye are able; but will with the temptation also make a way to escape, that ye may be able to bear it.

1 Corinthians 10:13

When you're in Christ, you have a safeguard. God is in control of your life. God will not put more on you than you can bear.[9] He doesn't need you to be a soft, weak, frail, or flimsy stalk. He needs a powerful, stalwart, massive, towering tree of strength. He doesn't want you soft. God doesn't want tinfoil or plastic armament. He wants steel.

One of the fundamental doctrines of the Church is the baptism of fire.[10] We understand baptism in water and the baptism of the Holy Ghost. John baptized in water. Jesus baptizes you with the Holy Ghost and with fire.

John answered, saying unto them all, I indeed baptize you with water; but one mightier than I cometh, the latchet of whose shoes I am not worthy to unloose: He shall baptize you with the Holy Ghost and with fire:

Whose fan is in His hand, and He will throughly purge His floor, and will gather the wheat into His garner; but the chaff He will burn with fire unquenchable.

Luke 3:16-17

He'll baptize you with the Holy Ghost and with fire. The fan is in God's hand. He separates the chaff from the wheat and burns it with fire unquenchable. God created the smith who blows the coals. He knows how much heat is needed in your life to make you what you have to be so He can use you for His glory. He won't put more fire on you than you can bear. He knows how much fire you can bear. If you couldn't take it, God wouldn't be blowing on it. He needs you to be broken, hurt, crushed, and bruised.

The devil can't hurt you because it is God who is fanning the fire. God is making it hot to remove that weak link in your armor. He knows just how hot the fire needs to be to strengthen you. When the devil attacks that weak spot with his weapons, he's surprised because God's arrows have already fixed it. God is the one who blew the coals[11] to make you a useful instrument in His hand.[12]

No captain who goes to war can properly lead his troops unless he's come back from battle with a wound somewhere.[13] Men aren't leaders because of their knowledge. Men follow leaders who have been in the blood, the guts, and the fire. We need leaders who know how to hurt. God doesn't need an army that has never been in the field or soldiers who have never fired a shot. God's army is composed of bleeding, hurting, wounded, and healed people.

The Baptism of Fire

And as the people were in expectation, and all men mused in their hearts of John, whether he were the Christ, or not;

John answered, saying unto them all, I indeed baptize you with water; but one mightier than I cometh, the latchet of whose shoes I am not worthy to unloose: He shall baptize you with the Holy Ghost and with fire:

Whose fan is in His hand, and He will throughly purge His floor, and will gather the wheat into His garner; but the chaff He will burn with fire unquenchable.

Luke 3:15-17

I am come to send fire on the earth; and what will I, if it be already kindled?

But I have a baptism to be baptized with; and how am I straitened till it be accomplished!

Suppose ye that I am come to give peace on earth? I tell you, Nay; but rather division:

For from henceforth there shall be five in one house divided, three against two and two against three.

The father shall be divided against the son, and the son against the father; the mother against the daughter, and the daughter against the mother; the mother in law against her daughter in law, and the daughter in law against her mother in law.

Luke 12:49-53

And Jesus being full of the Holy Ghost returned from Jordan, and was led by the Spirit into the wilderness,

Being forty days tempted of the devil. And in those days He did eat nothing: and when they were ended, He afterward hungered.

Luke 4:1-2

All the programs and activities that a church can plan will never save the young people or cause the church to grow. Social activities are good for fellowship, but they are worthless to the growth of the Kingdom of God. Activities, programs, buildings, and property cannot take the place of spiritual growth.[14]

A congregation does not grow because a new building is built or people are added. We are born of the water and of the spirit. We are baptized into the Body by the Spirit.

For by one Spirit are we all baptized into one body, whether we be Jews or Gentiles, whether we be bond or free; and have been all made to drink into one Spirit.

1 Corinthians 12:13

Moreover, brethren, I would not that ye should be ignorant, how that all our fathers were under the cloud, and all passed through the sea;

And were all baptized unto Moses in the cloud and in the sea;

And did all eat the same spiritual meat;

And did all drink the same spiritual drink: for they drank of that spiritual Rock that followed them: and that Rock was Christ.

1 Corinthians 10:1-4

The Church of the living God is the mother to the saints.[15] God is the Father that gives life to the Church. We are the sons and daughters of God.[16] We were all born to serve the Lord,[17] not to live in sin or iniquity outside of the law of the Spirit.

For the law of the Spirit of life in Christ Jesus hath made me free from the law of sin and death.

For what the law could not do, in that it was weak through the flesh, God sending His own Son in the likeness of sinful flesh, and for sin, condemned sin in the flesh:

That the righteousness of the law might be fulfilled in us, who walk not after the flesh, but after the Spirit.

For they that are after the flesh do mind the things of the flesh; but they that are after the Spirit the things of the Spirit.

For to be carnally minded is death; but to be spiritually minded is life and peace.

Because the carnal mind is enmity against God: for it is not subject to the law of God, neither indeed can be.

So then they that are in the flesh cannot please God.

But ye are not in the flesh, but in the Spirit, if so be that the Spirit of God dwell in you. Now if any man have not the Spirit of Christ, he is none of His.

Romans 8:2-9

There are some assumptions that we have made. We understand the baptism of the Holy Ghost.[18] We are the people who, in this century, originally received this gift and understand the outpouring[19] and operation of the Holy Ghost.[20] Denominational people who have received the Holy Ghost in recent months and years are told that we have been doing this for many years. We understand the baptism of the Holy Ghost.

The baptism of fire is not so easily assumed. There is something lacking in the Pentecostal experience. We preach a message that we do not live. We talk about the Book of Acts, but we do not do the things that are written there. We talk about power and about signs and wonders that we do not see. There is a sporadic dispensation of healings and miracles at times, but the constant flowing of miraculous activity described in the Scriptures as being a part of Christ's Church and Body is not present among us.[21]

But ye shall receive power, after that the Holy Ghost is come upon you: and ye shall be witnesses unto Me both in Jerusalem, and in all Judaea, and in Samaria, and unto the uttermost part of the earth.

Acts 1:8

There is a reason we are not endued with power. The Scripture doesn't say that we would receive power *when* the Holy Ghost comes upon us. It says we would receive power *after* the Holy Ghost comes upon us. Many years ago, people who preached sanctification[22] as a definite second work of grace knew about another baptism.

The baptism of the Holy Ghost is not the last gate in the journey between earth and Heaven. It is a birth into a life that should take us from glory to glory[23] and from faith to faith.[24] The Church needs more than the basic precepts.

Therefore leaving the principles of the doctrine of Christ, let us go on unto perfection; not laying again the foundation of repentance from dead works, and of faith toward God,

Of the doctrine of baptisms, and of laying on of hands, and of resurrection of the dead, and of eternal judgment.

Hebrews 6:1-2

The apostolic church in this century is not preaching this message. We need more than the baptism of the Holy Ghost— we need the baptism of fire.

We make a mistake when we assume that the baptism of fire is the excitement we get with the Holy Ghost, because fire crackles and burns. We say, "It's burning in my soul." The baptism of fire is not a baptism of joy and excitement. Jesus said, "I am come to send fire on the earth. What is it if it is already kindled?"[25] The fire was already burning because Jesus was there. It was burning in Jesus when He looked at

23

the Pharisees, and said, "...ye make clean the outside of the cup and of the platter, but within they are full of extortion and excess."[26] He burned them with His fire.

Woe unto you, scribes and Pharisees, hypocrites! for ye make clean the outside of the cup and of the platter, but within they are full of extortion and excess.

Thou blind Pharisee, cleanse first that which is within the cup and platter, that the outside of them may be clean also.

Woe unto you, scribes and Pharisees, hypocrites! for ye are like unto whited sepulchres, which indeed appear beautiful outward, but are within full of dead men's bones, and of all uncleanness.

Matthew 23:25-27

He answered and said unto them, Well hath Esaias prophesied of you hypocrites, as it is written, This people honoureth Me with their lips, but their heart is far from Me.

Mark 7:6

Jesus burned them, and the fire burned until they killed Him.[27] But killing Him didn't put the fire out.[28]

Then came to Him the mother of Zebedee's children with her sons, worshiping Him, and desiring a certain thing of Him.

And He said unto her, What wilt thou? She saith unto Him, Grant that these my two sons may sit, the one on Thy right hand, and the other on the left, in Thy kingdom.

But Jesus answered and said, Ye know not what ye ask. Are ye able to drink of the cup that I shall drink of, and to be baptized with the baptism that I am baptized with? They say unto Him, We are able.

And He saith unto them, Ye shall drink indeed of My cup, and be baptized with the baptism that I am baptized with: but to sit on My right hand, and on My left, is not Mine to give, but it shall be given to them for whom it is prepared of My Father.

Matthew 20:20-23

There is more to spiritual life than the baptism of the Holy Ghost. You must have consecration, dedication, and consistency to have the life of God. One Spirit baptizes us into the Body of Christ. Once we are in that Body we need the baptism of fire.

What was the cup that He was drinking of and what was the baptism that He was baptized with? He drank the cup in Gethsemane. The cross was His baptism.

Then cometh Jesus with them unto a place called Gethsemane, and saith unto the disciples, Sit ye here, while I go and pray yonder.

And He took with Him Peter and the two sons of Zebedee, and began to be sorrowful and very heavy.

Then saith He unto them, My soul is exceeding sorrowful, even unto death: tarry ye here, and watch with Me.

And He went a little farther, and fell on His face, and prayed, saying, O My Father, if it be possible, let this cup pass from Me: nevertheless not as I will, but as Thou wilt.

And He cometh unto the disciples, and findeth them asleep, and saith unto Peter, What, could ye not watch with Me one hour?

Watch and pray, that ye enter not into temptation: the spirit indeed is willing, but the flesh is weak.

> *He went away again the second time, and prayed,*
> *saying, O My Father, if this cup may not pass away*
> *from Me, except I drink it, Thy will be done.*
>
> Matthew 26:36-42

That cup was full of the sins of the whole world.[29] Every sin that had been committed from the very beginning of time, and every sin that would ever be committed, was in that cup.[30] That cup was brimming full, and the justice of God required that something be done about it. Jesus came to drink that cup for me.

If Jesus had drunk the cup without doing anything else, we would still not be redeemed. When He drank the cup, He accepted responsibility for all sin. Accepting responsibility does not take care of the problem. I cannot pay a mortgage just by assuming it. I still have to borrow the money and pay the note.

Drinking the cup didn't bring redemption. That was just an acknowledgment that He would take away the sin of the world.[31] That didn't take it away. He sealed the agreement by drinking the cup. He went to Calvary to pay the note. Calvary was the baptism of fire.

Endnotes—Chapter 2

1. Revelation 21:19; Isaiah 54:11
2. 1 Peter 1:7
3. 2 Timothy 1:7
4. Daniel 3:17
5. Isaiah 54:17
6. Isaiah 54:16
7. John 19:11
8. Isaiah 54:16
9. 1 Corinthians 10:13
10. Hebrews 6:2; Matthew 3:11; Luke 3:16
11. Isaiah 54:16
12. Isaiah 41:15; Romans 6:13
13. Hebrews 2:10
14. Ephesians 4:15; 1 Peter 3:18
15. Hebrews 12:22; Galatians 4:26
16. 1 John 3:1
17. Romans 6:19
18. Matthew 3:11; Mark 1:8; Luke 3:16; John 1:33; Acts 10:44-47; 11:15-16
19. Acts 2:4
20. 1 Corinthians 12:6
21. Acts 3:7; 5:5,10,15; 13:11; 14:3,10; 16:18; 19:11; 20:10; 28:5,11
22. 2 Thessalonians 2:13
23. 2 Corinthians 3:18
24. 1 Corinthians 10:15; 2 Thessalonians 1:3

25. Luke 12:49
26. Matthew 23:25
27. Acts 2:23
28. Acts 5:28
29. 1 John 2:2
30. Psalm 75:8
31. John 1:29

Chapter 3

Let the Fire Burn

Though He were a Son, yet learned He obedience by the things which He suffered.

Hebrews 5:8

Wherefore Jesus also, that He might sanctify the people with His own blood, suffered without the gate.

Let us go forth therefore unto Him without the camp, bearing His reproach.

Hebrews 13:12-13

Forasmuch then as Christ hath suffered for us in the flesh, arm yourselves likewise with the same mind: for he that hath suffered in the flesh hath ceased from sin;

That he no longer should live the rest of his time in the flesh to the lusts of men, but to the will of God.

1 Peter 4:1-2

You cannot bear the cross without suffering.[1]

I am crucified with Christ: nevertheless I live; yet not I, but Christ liveth in me: and the life which I now live in the flesh I live by the faith of the Son of God, who loved me, and gave Himself for me.

Galatians 2:20

29

> *But what things were gain to me, those I counted loss for Christ.*
>
> *Yea doubtless, and I count all things but loss for the excellency of the knowledge of Christ Jesus my Lord: for whom I have suffered the loss of all things, and do count them but dung, that I may win Christ.*
>
> Philippians 3:7-8

This is not something that comes simply from the Holy Ghost baptism. Paul loved the gospel and the cause of Christ so much that nothing he physically owned, and nothing that he had learned meant anything compared to his personal desire to give himself unequivocally and unsolicited to God, with "no strings attached."[2]

Suffering was part of that offering. Paul was attacked by beasts at Ephesus,[3] stoned at Lystra,[4] and beaten many times.[5] When he was in prison, he didn't grumble and complain against the cross.[6] He was dead to the flesh and alive to God.[7] When they let him out of prison, he didn't go to a retirement home, but to the executioner's block.

> *For I am now ready to be offered, and the time of my departure is at hand.*
>
> *I have fought a good fight, I have finished my course, I have kept the faith:*
>
> *Henceforth there is laid up for me a crown of righteousness, which the Lord, the righteous judge, shall give me at that day: and not to me only, but unto all them also that love His appearing.*
>
> 2 Timothy 4:6-8

We immunize ourselves from suffering. We dread the cross. We do not like the pit. We hate shackles and bonds. Sacrifice is something we have to make ourselves do because the baptism of fire has never seared our flesh. Fire burns all the nerves until it extinguishes their ability to feel.

John the Baptist said God's fire would thoroughly purge His threshing floor. He will burn up everything that is not good and right. We need the baptism of fire to burn up everything in our lives that is not right. Let the fire burn the chaff.[8]

We need a baptism of fire to burn up the nervous systems of fleshly desire and materialism so the sirens of this time will not be able to draw us away from the old rugged cross. Discouragement and deception are the problems of the day. If we suffered as we should, we wouldn't have time to think about those things. The pain would be enough.

It is a shame that we have to be reminded to pray, coaxed to read the Bible, and asked to come to church. We need a baptism of fire to burn the hardness off of our hearts.

The church under fire is the only church that has ever grown. People had their eyes plucked out by ravens. Their children were sawn asunder, they were stripped naked, stretched out and spread-eagled in front of them, and hot tar was dropped on their mid-sections while they screamed in torture, while the parents watched helplessly from their position, tethered to poles.[9] Fingers, toes, and other organs were cut from their bodies with a dull knife while they screamed for their parents to deliver them. One word from their parents denying that Christ was the Lord would have saved their children. Those parents loved their babies as much as you love your babies, but they held their tongues and let them die, screaming with misunderstanding because their parents loved not their lives unto death.[10] Husbands didn't spare wives and wives didn't spare husbands.

All that suffering never stopped the march of the Church.[11] The church under fire is a church that can grow. The church that suffers can live. The church that has suffered with Him shall reign with Him.[12]

There's no fire in the Church today. There's a lot of Holy Ghost, but no fire. We can shout but we have no power.

And Abraham rose up early in the morning, and saddled his ass, and took two of his young men with him, and Isaac his son, and clave the wood for the burnt offering, and rose up, and went unto the place of which God had told him.

Then on the third day Abraham lifted up his eyes, and saw the place afar off.

And Abraham said unto his young men, Abide ye here with the ass; and I and the lad will go yonder and worship, and come again to you.

And Abraham took the wood of the burnt offering, and laid it upon Isaac his son; and he took the fire in his hand, and a knife; and they went both of them together.

And Isaac spake unto Abraham his father, and said, My father: and he said, Here am I, my son. And he said, Behold the fire and the wood: but where is the lamb for a burnt offering?

And Abraham said, My son, God will provide Himself a lamb for a burnt offering: so they went both of them together.

Genesis 22:3-8

It was a three-day journey for Abraham to go to Moriah.[13] When he approached close enough to see the place where he would offer his son, he told the servants to stay with the beasts. He was going to worship. Is it worship to kill your son? It is always worship when you do what God says to do, and give up the things that God wants. Abraham's adoration for God was greater than his personal parental feeling for his own flesh. His love for God was more than humanity could deserve.

Abraham laid the wood on the boy's back and carried the fire in his hand. The boy saw the wood and the fire, but he didn't see the sacrifice. We have wood, and we go up in smoke when the Holy Ghost falls, but we will not sacrifice ourselves when the fire comes down. The fire burns the wood, but we save ourselves. We give Him wood, but we won't give Him ourselves. That's why we have a lot of smoke.

We don't mind giving God words. Sometimes we'll give Him time. We'll even give Him a little money. We won't give Him our hearts and travail in intercessory prayer before the Lord.

And be found in Him, not having mine own righteousness, which is of the law, but that which is through the faith of Christ, the righteousness which is of God by faith:

That I may know Him, and the power of His resurrection, and the fellowship of His sufferings, being made conformable unto His death.

Philippians 3:9-10

The fire burns chaff and purges the floor.[14] It burns up every bit of dross and purifies the gold and silver.[15] Every soul that makes it to glory will be tried by fire.[16] There will not be one soul in God's Kingdom who has not gone to the fire.

Every man's work shall be made manifest: for the day shall declare it, because it shall be revealed by fire; and the fire shall try every man's work of what sort it is.

If any man's work abide which he hath built thereupon, he shall receive a reward.

If any man's work shall be burned, he shall suffer loss: but he himself shall be saved; yet so as by fire.

1 Corinthians 3:13-15

Yea, and all that will live godly in Christ Jesus shall suffer persecution.

2 Timothy 3:12

Do you know what gives the Church power? Power comes when the Church dies to itself. Jesus didn't get power when He drank the cup or when He was committed to doing the will of God. Jesus got power when He died to Himself. When He hung on the cross and said, "It is finished," the heavens lit up with lightning and the skies darkened.[17] Thunder reigned supreme. Graves were opened.[18]

God's Church is not a social church. God's Church is a church that is completely sold out. The Church is no place for gossips to hang out. The Church is a marching army of dedicated people who do not consider themselves.[19] They are not ashamed of the gospel of Christ.[20] They love not their lives unto death.[21] They have no attachments to this world.[22] Money cannot buy them.[23] They do not become discouraged. God holds them in the hollow of His hand. No man can pluck them out of His hand.[24]

God's Church is a Holy Ghost entity that cannot be put together with the doctrines of men.[25] Without the Spirit, there is no Church. There's nothing to live for without the fire.

For since I spake, I cried out, I cried violence and spoil; because the word of the Lord was made a reproach unto me, and a derision, daily.

Then I said, I will not make mention of Him, nor speak any more in His name. But His word was in mine heart as a burning fire shut up in my bones, and I was weary with forbearing, and I could not stay.

Jeremiah 20:8-9

The baptism of fire will burn you out of your corner and place you where you need to be with God. It will burn up the chaff in your life.

Social people don't like you to talk about standards. They don't like you to preach against sin. They want to live just as close to the world as they can and as close to God as they can.[26] This world is eaten up with iniquity. The spirit of iniquity is already working and some of it is in the Church.[27] The Church doesn't like preaching about living and acting right because it makes the congregation suffer a little bit.

We need to put the flesh in its place and prove that God is God, and that we love Him more than we love our flesh.[28] We need to incinerate the things that we don't need when those things are probable danger spots. Even if you could do whatever you wanted to and still live for God, that doesn't mean that you should.[29] Those are the seeds of iniquity.

God's Church is a holy, disciplined church tried by fire.

People who have suffered have ceased from sin.[30] Doing without things you could have is suffering.[31] Fasting is suffering. We need to die to the flesh and be crucified with Christ.[32]

People baptized by fire can make it anywhere because they don't need much. Little things destroy people whom the fire has not seared. They're still alive in the flesh; they are not dead to the world. They can lie and cheat and get by, thinking everything is all right. It doesn't bother them to do those things because they can reason it out.

God's Church is sold out to His name.[33] They love God first and everything else comes second. They do whatever He says without a second thought.[34] God's Church has grown far beyond its birth. You don't have to rock its members in their cradle to keep them saved. They're baptized with fire. They're not afraid to suffer in the flesh.

We need to stop praying for mercy and deliverance from the fire and start praying for the fire. People don't appreciate mercy unless they have been baptized with fire. Some people may lose their souls because you prayed for mercy to fall on them when the fire would bring them to salvation. It is an injustice to hold out mercy and not let the fire burn.

Pain will make you more prayerful. Heartache and travail will make us more faithful. Loneliness will make you love your neighbor more.[35] The loss of all things will make you see souls.[36]

"Are you able...to be baptized with the baptism that I am baptized with?" (Mt. 20:22)

"...and the fire shall try every man's work..." (1 Cor. 3:13).

A lady asked me to pray for her husband to be saved because he was lost and didn't want God. She said she would give anything for him to be saved. This couple was very wealthy—they had a chicken farm that did good business. "Would you be willing to lose everything for him to be saved?" I asked. She said that she would.

God took her at her word. The next night everything they had burned to the ground. All the chickens and the barns were destroyed. The garage caught on fire and burned their cars. They didn't have any money because it was hidden on the farm and it burned. They lost everything in one night.

Although they had good insurance, the policy had lapsed by one day. They lost everything without an insurance policy. When they took the insurance company to court, they lost the case. The lady asked for prayer that God would give them back their farm, their cars, and their money. I reminded her that she had prayed that God would save her husband at any cost. She turned and walked away.

Holy Ghost people love Him for His benefits.[37] They follow Him for the loaves and the fishes.[38] As long as He's blessing, they hold their hands out and talk about His goodness. When Jesus wants us to eat His flesh and drink His blood, they pack up and leave.[39] Can you drink from the cup that He drinks and be baptized with the baptism that He is baptized with?

Endnotes—Chapter 3

1. Luke 9:23
2. Philippians 3:8
3. 1 Corinthians 15:32
4. Acts 14:5
5. 2 Corinthians 11:24-25
6. Acts 20:24; Philippians 3:7; 4:11
7. Romans 6:11
8. Luke 3:17
9. Hebrews 11:35-37
10. Revelation 2:10; 12:11
11. Acts 8:1,4
12. 2 Timothy 2:12
13. Genesis 22:1,4
14. Proverbs 25:4; Isaiah 1:25
15. 1 Peter 1:7
16. Revelation 7:14
17. Matthew 27:45,51
18. Matthew 27:52
19. Philippians 2:4
20. Romans 1:16
21. Revelation 12:11
22. 1 John 2:15; Matthew 6:19-21
23. 1 Timothy 6:10
24. John 10:28-29
25. Mark 7:7; Hebrews 13:9

26. Matthew 6:24
27. 2 Thessalonians 2:4,7
28. Galatians 6:8
29. 1 Corinthians 6:12
30. 1 Peter 4:1
31. Colossians 3:5; Romans 8:13
32. Galatians 2:20
33. James 1:27; Romans 12:2; 1 John 5:19
34. Colossians 3:17
35. Romans 12:20
36. Philippians 3:8
37. Psalm 103:2
38. John 6:26
39. John 6:53,66

Chapter 4

The Process
Come With Me to the
Sacrifice

And the Lord said unto Samuel, How long wilt thou mourn for Saul, seeing I have rejected him from reigning over Israel? fill thine horn with oil, and go, I will send thee to Jesse the Bethlehemite: for I have provided Me a king among his sons.

And Samuel said, How can I go? if Saul hear it, he will kill me. And the Lord said, Take an heifer with thee, and say, I am come to sacrifice to the Lord.

And call Jesse to the sacrifice, and I will shew thee what thou shalt do: and thou shalt anoint unto Me him whom I name unto thee.

And Samuel did that which the Lord spake, and came to Bethlehem. And the elders of the town trembled at his coming, and said, Comest thou peaceably?

And he said, Peaceably: I am come to sacrifice unto the Lord: sanctify yourselves, and come with me to the sacrifice. And he sanctified Jesse and his sons, and called them to the sacrifice.

And it came to pass, when they were come, that he looked on Eliab, and said, Surely the Lord's anointed is before Him.

But the Lord said unto Samuel, Look not on his countenance, or on the height of his stature; because I have refused him: for the Lord seeth not as man seeth; for man looketh on the outward appearance, but the Lord looketh on the heart.

Then Jesse called Abinadab, and made him pass before Samuel. And he said, Neither hath the Lord chosen this.

Then Jesse made Shammah to pass by. And he said, Neither hath the Lord chosen this.

Again, Jesse made seven of his sons to pass before Samuel. And Samuel said unto Jesse, The Lord hath not chosen these.

And Samuel said unto Jesse, Are here all thy children? And he said, There remaineth yet the youngest, and, behold, he keepeth the sheep. And Samuel said unto Jesse, Send and fetch him: for we will not sit down till he come hither.

And he sent, and brought him in. Now he was ruddy, and withal of a beautiful countenance, and goodly to look to. And the Lord said, Arise, anoint him: for this is he.

Then Samuel took the horn of oil, and anointed him in the midst of his brethren: and the Spirit of the Lord came upon David from that day forward. So Samuel rose up, and went to Ramah.

1 Samuel 16:1-13

When the holy God of Heaven becomes aligned with our spirits so that we humanly manifest His Deity, that is the anointing. When you sing, it isn't your song—it's His song.

When you're preaching, it's not your sermon—it's His word. When you witness, it's not your experience—it's God's life manifested through you. The anointing is the very essence of God.

"No man hath seen God at any time; the only begotten Son, which is in the bosom of the Father, He hath declared Him" (Jn. 1:18).

We cannot look at Him. Two millenniums have not erased the glory of His earthly presence. Have you ever wished you could see Him? You have to see Him through His Word.[1] You have to hear Him in a song. You have to hear Him in a message. You have to love Him in somebody's praise. One day we will see Him as He is in all His glory, but now we have to live for the anointing.

The Old Testament priests expressed the anointing first. Then the prophets expressed it. The oil, which was a type of the Spirit, expressed the anointing.[2] The ram's horn held the oil for special events or when someone was to be specially used.[3]

One of the first things of the covenant was the preparation of the anointing oil.[4] The olives were to be beaten. There was a specific formula to be followed when mixing the anointing oil. There had to be a fragrance and an essence. The eyes had to see it. The nostrils had to smell it. The hands could touch it. It was the expression of what would come to the Church in Jesus Christ. He will anoint us with the glory and the gladness of His presence.[5] The essence of Christ is in His body. The anointing is precious.

When God anointed a prophet, the anointing set him apart. The anointing is an alignment. God gives us His essence. The prophets had to have the essence of God to see.[6]

Otherwise, they could only see as far as mortal eyes could see and direct as far as minds of men could direct. With divine direction, the prophet prophesies as one who sees with the sight of God.[7] Things that angels wish to do are in our songs. The essence is here.

Samuel was taken when he was a very small boy. He grew up in the back of the church. His mother had taken him to the church and handed him over to Eli, the priest.[8] She had promised in that very place to lend her son to the Lord for life if God would only give her a son to lend.[9]

The Bible says Eli marked her face.[10] That means he made a special note of her because of her deep sobbing. When he noticed her lips were moving, but heard no words, he chastised her for being drunk in the church. She wasn't drunk. She had poured out her soul unto the Lord. When he finally understood, Eli said, "The Lord grant thee thy petition ."

She didn't give Samuel to the Lord. She lent him to the Lord. She kept the part to pray for him. She kept those rights. A prayer that can open a barren womb is worthy to pray for a lonely boy in the back of a church. She may have been praying for him when he first heard the Lord call his name.

And the child Samuel ministered unto the Lord before Eli. And the word of the Lord was precious in those days; there was no open vision.

And it came to pass at that time, when Eli was laid down in his place, and his eyes began to wax dim, that he could not see;

And ere the lamp of God went out in the temple of the Lord, where the ark of God was, and Samuel was laid down to sleep;

That the Lord called Samuel: and he answered, Here am I.

And he ran unto Eli, and said, Here am I; for thou call-edst me. And he said, I called not; lie down again. And he went and lay down.

And the Lord called yet again, Samuel. And Samuel arose and went to Eli, and said, Here am I; for thou didst call me. And he answered, I called not, my son; lie down again.

Now Samuel did not yet know the Lord, neither was the word of the Lord yet revealed unto him.

And the Lord called Samuel again the third time. And he arose and went to Eli, and said, Here am I; for thou didst call me. And Eli perceived that the Lord had called the child.

Therefore Eli said unto Samuel, Go, lie down: and it shall be, if He call thee, that thou shalt say, Speak, Lord; for Thy servant heareth. So Samuel went and lay down in his place.

1 Samuel 3:1-9

The Lord raised Samuel to be a mighty prophet. Not one word that Samuel spoke ever fell to the ground.[11] Everything that he ever said came to pass. The men in Bethlehem were trembling when that old man came with his perspiration-polished staff and deep hoary eyes. His word was God's word. Whatever he said was what God was saying.

The only time that Samuel ever tried to circumvent the word of God was when he was sent to anoint a king. Samuel did everything God told him to do without question until he came to Jesse's house.

God told Samuel to stop mourning over Saul. Samuel still remembered the tall kid that they had to drag out from under the chariot wheel.[12] Saul was a humble child from Kish's house.[13] The people shouted, "God save the king."[14] God did His best to save that king. Saul wouldn't let God save him. He went downhill from that moment. He had a humble beginning. Now he wanted to be priest as well as king.[15] Now he was invading the holy things of God. He doesn't have any patience for God or the man of God.

God felt disgust for Saul.[16] Samuel's tender heart was still bleeding for the boy he had anointed. God told him not to grieve over him any more. God had found another boy. God told him to take his horn, fill it with oil, and anoint another king. The very essence of Deity was upon him.

Samuel said he couldn't do it. He said Saul would kill him. Why was he afraid of Saul? None of his words fell to the ground. He could speak one word and Saul would be dead.

Time and peer pressure sometimes make us all tremble. God made a way for him. All he had to do to escape the wrath of Saul was take a heifer, and say, "Come with me to the sacrifice."

Did God have to create a ruse just to get past one man? God put 150 billion galaxies into proper orbit in space. The sun is in just the right place, 93 billion miles away, to give us heat and not burn us up. God knew that. God can make a tree grow out of black soil. He can make a black and white cow give creamy butter and milk by eating green grass. He fashions the face of a child with His own fingers.

Samuel knew he was going to Bethlehem to anoint a king. God told him to say he was going to sacrifice. Anointing is power.[17] Anointing is God. Sacrifice is bloody death. Sacrifice is weakness. Sacrifice was given because we couldn't reach God. Sacrifice and the shedding of blood was an acceptable way to get us closer.[18] Why should the Almighty God have to avoid Saul? Does God have to fib to get by a crooked king?

He didn't. It was true that Samuel was going to sacrifice. That is the deeper meaning of anointing. People favor glory, but they don't like the offering that it takes to pay for it.

When we receive anointing, sacrifice comes with it. You become so lost in the presence and the essence of God.

"Then said Jesus unto His disciples, If any man will come after Me, let him deny himself, and take up his cross, and follow Me" (Mt. 16:24).

Samuel discovered there was a sacrifice that came with the oil. Everybody loves the anointing. It's more than speed and spit. The essence of God is a precious thing. Many have touched it a time or two, but blessed is he who lives in prayer enough to roll the sky back enough to live with the essence of His power, momentarily, day by day.

David stood beside his jealous brothers with the oil on his head. He was in the back of the pasture keeping his father's sheep, playing his harp, and writing songs when Eliab came for him.[19] Eliab wasn't happy about it. All his brothers lined up, and the old prophet poured the oil on David's head.

David didn't know what was happening. He was only a child. It was 15 years before he knew what happened. He lost Jonathan, his precious friend.[20] He hid from Saul in the cave of Adullam. He saw his cities burned with fire.[21] His wives were taken from him.[22] He pretended to be a mad man so the

Philistines would not know he was the mighty David who had removed the head of their mighty Goliath.[23] He had the essence of God, but he was also called to the sacrifice. He had to put his heart and his shoulder to the wheel.

His son was to be a Messiah who would sit on the throne of His father David forever.[24] In his youth, David was running from Saul.[25] In his old age, he was gathering material for a temple that he would not be able to build.[26] This man saw Christ in all His glory from His birth to His death and resurrection.[27]

I have set the Lord always before me: because He is at my right hand, I shall not be moved.

Therefore my heart is glad, and my glory rejoiceth: my flesh also shall rest in hope.

For Thou wilt not leave my soul in hell; neither wilt Thou suffer Thine Holy One to see corruption.

Psalm 16:8-10

David became the source for the foundational prophecy in the message that started the Church.

God denied him the right to build the temple.

Now it was in the heart of David my father to build an house for the name of the Lord God of Israel.

But the Lord said to David my father, Forasmuch as it was in thine heart to build an house for My name, thou didst well in that it was in thine heart:

Notwithstanding thou shalt not build the house....

2 Chronicles 6:7-9

Loneliness goes with the anointing. Was David doing the will of God when he cut off his enemies' heads?[28] Was he doing the will of God when he conquered all of Israel's enemies?[29] Did he do the will of God? Yes, he paid dearly for doing God's will.

David didn't just receive the anointing. He also slew the heifer and made the sacrifice.

There is a geometry in the cross that the twentieth-century Church must display. One parallel bar in the perimeter called the anointing is not enough to hold the steadfast Christ to a dying world. If there is only one vertical pole on the cross, you can nail His feet to the cross, but His face will lie on the ground before the world in humiliation. There has to be a horizontal bar. If you change that reality, you have lifeless religion. The vertical bar points God-ward, but the horizontal bar pulls His arms apart, exposes His heart, and gives His love. There must be opposition in the cross.[30] Some Christian men try to be like other men on the job because they do not want to offend them. It is necessary to offend them. If you fail to offend them, you change the geometry of the cross. There is always an offense.

There must be sacrifice with the anointing and great glory. You must carry the cross daily. If you can't bear the cross, you can't wear the crown.[31] If you anoint a boy who will be a man after God's own heart, you have to take a heifer to sacrifice.[32] In order for there to be anointing, there has to be sacrifice. They come together.

And, behold, two of them went that same day to a village called Emmaus, which was from Jerusalem about threescore furlongs.

And they talked together of all these things which had happened.

And it came to pass, that, while they communed together and reasoned, Jesus Himself drew near, and went with them.

But their eyes were holden that they should not know Him.

And He said unto them, What manner of communications are these that ye have one to another, as ye walk, and are sad?

And the one of them, whose name was Cleopas, answering said unto Him, Art Thou only a stranger in Jerusalem, and hast not known the things which are come to pass there in these days?

And He said unto them, What things? And they said unto Him, Concerning Jesus of Nazareth, which was a prophet mighty in deed and word before God and all the people:

And how the chief priests and our rulers delivered Him to be condemned to death, and have crucified Him.

But we trusted that it had been He which should have redeemed Israel: and beside all this, to day is the third day since these things were done.

Yea, and certain women also of our company made us astonished, which were early at the sepulchre;

And when they found not His body, they came, saying, that they had also seen a vision of angels, which said that He was alive.

And certain of them which were with us went to the sepulchre, and found it even so as the women had said: but Him they saw not.

Then He said unto them, O fools, and slow of heart to believe all that the prophets have spoken:

Ought not Christ to have suffered these things, and to enter into His glory?

And beginning at Moses and all the prophets, He expounded unto them in all the scriptures the things concerning Himself.

And they drew nigh unto the village, whither they went: and He made as though He would have gone further.

But they constrained Him, saying, Abide with us: for it is toward evening, and the day is far spent. And He went in to tarry with them.

And it came to pass, as He sat at meat with them, He took bread, and blessed it, and brake, and gave to them.

And their eyes were opened, and they knew Him; and He vanished out of their sight.

And they said one to another, Did not our heart burn within us, while He talked with us by the way, and while He opened to us the scriptures?

And they rose up the same hour, and returned to Jerusalem, and found the eleven gathered together, and them that were with them,

Saying, The Lord is risen indeed, and hath appeared to Simon.

And they told what things were done in the way, and how He was known of them in breaking of bread.

Luke 24:13-35

This passage of Scripture takes place in the shadow of the most glorious event in the Christian testimony, the cross of Christ.

"For the preaching of the cross is to them that perish foolishness; but unto us which are saved it is the power of God" (1 Cor. 1:18).

After Christ was scourged and bludgeoned, each of the 614 rough soldiers with calloused hands took their opportunity to issue a rough blow to His face.[33] They plucked out His beard.[34] He had bloody splotches on His cheeks and chin where they had pulled the hair out of the pores of His face. He had rubbery mucous hanging from His face from the throats of angry people who had spit on Him. He hung from that tree, tortured, His back looking like a plowed field from the lashing He'd received with the cat-o'-nine-tails. When they hit Him, they dragged the whip along His spine so that all nine pieces of leather lined with jagged pieces of metal and bone were like a cat clawing all the way to His abdomen.[35]

He hung on that cross, moving back and forth trying to escape the different types of pain that filled His muscles, cramping from this bizarre position.[36] He used His legs to push His back away from the scratchy tree but the cramps in His legs forced Him to fall right back into it. Every time His head fell back against that tree, it pushed the thorns deeper into His scalp.[37]

Isaiah had spoken of Him 730 years before He was born.

"As many were astonied [astonished] at Thee; His visage was so marred more than any man, and His form more than the sons of men" (Is. 52:14).

"He is despised and rejected of men; a man of sorrows, and acquainted with grief: and we hid as it were our faces from Him; He was despised, and we esteemed Him not" (Is. 53:3).

He was not pleasant to behold.

At a nod of His head, angels would have removed Him from the nails to some celestial portal and succored Him, but He refused to do that.[38] He died there. It was finished.[39]

It wasn't just finished for Jesus. It was finished for every disciple who loved Him and in the minds of each of them who adored Him. Every one who had seen Him do a miracle wondered if it had been real. How could someone who could take one boy's lunch bucket and feed 5,000 men die this way?[40]

Two of the disciples went to Emmaus. They were leaving hope and possibility on their way home from miracles, signs, and wonders. They reasoned together of those things which had happened.

Jesus drew near and went with them but their eyes "were holden that they should not know Him." He did not hide from them. He did not cover His face so they could not see Him.

"After that He appeared in another form unto two of them, as they walked, and went into the country. And they went and told it unto the residue: neither believed they them" (Mk. 16:12-13).

He appeared unto them and, as they looked at Him, they could not believe His shape. When they looked at Him, they could not believe He was Jesus. They failed to recognize Him because they were convinced He was dead. Because they saw Him on the cross, wrapped Him for burial, put spices on Him, and laid Him in a tomb,[41] they could not recognize or consider this living person to be Jesus. Their pain blinded them.

Preconceived ideas blind the whole Church. The Church cannot see Jesus because we have determined how He has to look and how He must appear. Some people cannot worship unless you play a particular style of music. Rhythm patterns reflect whether they will worship. Music determines whether something is Jesus to them. Some people cannot worship with white people because they are the wrong color. Some cannot worship with black people because they are the wrong color. Some people are caught up in ideology, thinking God is only in one place, time, or philosophy. They cannot see Jesus even though He is there.

Wise men see Him in a baby's smile, a thunderclap, or streaking in yellow lightning. A wise man can hear Him in the breath of a hummingbird or see Him in the mighty flight of an eagle.

These two men were reasoning. Jesus asked them what they were talking about. They asked Jesus if He was a stranger. He could have told them He was the one on the middle cross.

"We trusted that it had been He who should have redeemed Israel."

They were mad at Him because He should have delivered Israel.[42] His glory had lifted them up and His power had given them hope. If He could heal a blind man,[43] they knew He could deliver Israel from its national crisis. He could cast out the Gentiles and make Israel an independent nation.

"When they therefore were come together, they asked of Him, saying, Lord, wilt Thou at this time restore again the kingdom to Israel?" (Acts 1:6)

Their expectation was that at any time He would ride a white stallion, leading 12 other stallions, into Herod's temple, pull it down, and set it on fire.[44] Then they would go to Rome and get back at all the Romans who had been taxing them.[45] All they could think about was their national condition. They wanted to get rid of the Gentiles.[46]

He was transfigured on a mountain with Moses on one side of Him and Elijah on the other.[47] The disciples should have been listening instead of dreaming.[48] The topic of conversation was "His decease" which would be accomplished at Jerusalem.

"And, behold, there talked with Him two men, which were Moses and Elias: who appeared in glory, and spake of His decease which He should accomplish at Jerusalem" (Lk. 9:30-31).

He talked to them about dying on a cross on a hill in a town called Jerusalem.[49] He talked to Moses and Elijah about how He would die and the result of His death. The disciples were so caught up in the excitement of the event that they failed to hear what He was saying.

Moses represented the Law,[50] Elijah represented the prophets,[51] and Jesus fulfilled them both on a tree. Moses would tell Him what it was like to die before the glory because Moses died without ever going into the Promised Land.[52] Jesus had to go through the death of the cross before He would ever see any glory.[53] Elijah knew what it was like to be carried up into Heaven alive.[54] Jesus would be resurrected and caught up to Heaven.[55]

The disciples should have listened to what Jesus was saying. He explained His crucifixion and resurrection to them repeatedly.[56] They did not understand what He said.[57] His power blinded them.

They had an earthly kingdom on their minds and they wouldn't hear anything else. They didn't understand anything else. When He died, their dreams died and they lost their faith in what He had done.

Endnotes—Chapter 4

1. John 1:1,14
2. Exodus 90:15
3. 2 Samuel 22:3; Luke 1:69; 1 Samuel 16:13; 2:1
4. Exodus 30:22-28; 37:29
5. Psalm 45:7; Hebrews 1:9
6. 1 Samuel 9:9
7. Numbers 24:3
8. 1 Samuel 1:24-28
9. 1 Samuel 1:11
10. 1 Samuel 1:12
11. 1 Samuel 3:19
12. 1 Samuel 10:22
13. 1 Samuel 9:1-2
14. 1 Samuel 10:24
15. 1 Samuel 13:9
16. 1 Samuel 16:1
17. Isaiah 10:27
18. Hebrews 9:22; Leviticus 17:11; Matthew 26:28
19. 1 Samuel 16:11; Psalm 78:70-71
20. 2 Samuel 1:4
21. 1 Samuel 30:1
22. 1 Samuel 30:5
23. 1 Samuel 21:13
24. 1 Chronicles 17:11-14
25. 1 Samuel 23:25-26

26. 1 Chronicles 22:7-8
27. Acts 2:29-36
28. 1 Samuel 17:46,51
29. 1 Chronicles 18
30. John 16:2
31. 2 Timothy 4:8; 1 Corinthians 9:25
32. 1 Samuel 13:14
33. Luke 22:64
34. Isaiah 50:6
35. Isaiah 53:5; 1 Peter 2:24
36. Psalm 22:14-16
37. Mark 15:17
38. Psalm 91:11; Matthew 4:6; Luke 4:10
39. John 19:30
40. John 6:9; Mark 6:44
41. Mark 15:46; Luke 23:53-56; John 19:38-42
42. Acts 1:6
43. John 9:1-41
44. Revelation 19:11-14; Mark 13:1-2
45. Mark 12:13-17
46. Acts 11:1-3
47. Matthew 17:3
48. Matthew 17:22-23
49. Matthew 16:21
50. Mark 1:44
51. Malachi 4:5

52. Deuteronomy 32:48-52
53. Hebrews 12:2
54. 2 Kings 2:11
55. 1 Corinthians 15:4; Acts 1:9
56. Matthew 16:21; 17:22-23; 20:19
57. Matthew 13:15

Chapter 5

The Process
The Order of Breaking Bread

Then He said unto them, O fools, and slow of heart to believe all that the prophets have spoken:

Ought not Christ to have suffered these things, and to enter into His glory?

And beginning at Moses and all the prophets, He expounded unto them in all the scriptures the things concerning Himself...

...He took bread, and blessed it, and brake, and gave to them.

And their eyes were opened, and they knew Him..."

Luke 24:25-27; 30-31

If you have spent enough time with someone, you immediately recognize him even if you have not seen him in a long time, even if he has facial surgery. They should have recognized Jesus by His conversation or the sound of His voice.[1] They should have known Jesus by His countenance. They should have been able to recognize Him by His stature and the gait of His walk, and say, "That's Jesus." They had been with Him three years. They should have known Him by the way He walked. They should have recognized that swing in His left arm.

My sheep hear My voice, and I know them, and they follow Me.

John 10:27

And a stranger will they not follow, but will flee from him: for they know not the voice of strangers.

John 10:5

But Mary stood without at the sepulchre weeping: and as she wept, she stooped down, and looked into the sepulchre,

And seeth two angels in white sitting, the one at the head, and the other at the feet, where the body of Jesus had lain.

And they say unto her, Woman, why weepest thou? She saith unto them, Because they have taken away my Lord, and I know not where they have laid Him.

And when she had thus said, she turned herself back, and saw Jesus standing, and knew not that it was Jesus.

Jesus saith unto her, Woman, why weepest thou? whom seekest thou? She, supposing Him to be the gardener, saith unto Him, Sir, if Thou have borne Him hence, tell me where Thou hast laid Him, and I will take Him away.

Jesus saith unto her, Mary. She turned herself, and saith unto Him, Rabboni; which is to say, Master.

John 20:11-16

Mary recognized Jesus by His voice. Sometimes women are more sensitive than men. Women respond quicker. They have a lower threshold in their yielding point. They can say, "Yes" quicker. She recognized Him by the way He said, "Mary." That's all it took.

On the road to Emmaus, the disciples should have known Jesus by His countenance, His conversation, or His message. For seven-and-one-half miles, He talked of no one but Himself.

I would have liked to have been on that road. Jesus started at the very beginning with Adam and Eve[2] and spoke all the things that Moses and the prophets spoke about Him. They must have discussed 22,000 references to the Messiah on this journey. He wouldn't leave out one reference or leave one Scripture unquoted.

They should have snapped out of formality, organizational settings, religious systems, and ideologies, and entered into reality. His presence should have broken through it, but the power of men's systems is strong. It keeps people from power, recognition, and knowing God.

Preconceived ideas blinded them as they blind the Church today.[3] Blindness to further revelation blinds many Pentecostal and Charismatic people today because they cannot see past their conception of Him.

"Then He said unto them, O fools, and slow of heart to believe all that the prophets have spoken: ought not Christ to have suffered these things, and to enter into His glory?" (Lk. 24:25-26)

They should have recognized that because He had done it before. "Woe unto you, scribes and Pharisees, hypocrites! for ye make clean the outside of the cup and of the platter, but within they are full of extortion and excess."[4] They were whited sepulchres shined up on the outside but full of dead men's bones inside.[5] That sounds a lot like "O fools!"

He told them they should have believed "all." Religion has nailed us because we have become satisfied with less than "all." They didn't get the whole story. They heard only the glory part, where He rides the white horse[6] and rules the nations with a rod of iron.[7]

One school of the Hebrews said He would be *Messiah Ben-judah*, the reigning king. They would tell you the King of glory would conquer the gates of hell, rule with a rod of iron on the throne of David,[8] and lead the kingdoms of Heaven and earth.[9]

> *Lift up your heads, O ye gates; and be ye lift up, ye ever-lasting doors; and the King of glory shall come in.*
>
> *Who is this King of glory? The Lord strong and mighty, the Lord mighty in battle.*
>
> *Lift up your heads, O ye gates; even lift them up, ye ever-lasting doors; and the King of glory shall come in.*
>
> *Who is this King of glory? The Lord of hosts, He is the King of glory. Selah.*

Psalms 24:7-10

Another school of the Hebrews said He was *Messiah Ben-Yosef*. Joseph was in a pit[10] and a dungeon.[11] Joseph was in Potiphar's house.[12] He was the suffering savior. That is who their Messiah was.

> *But He was wounded for our transgressions, He was bruised for our iniquities: the chastisement of our peace was upon Him; and with His stripes we are healed.*
>
> *All we like sheep have gone astray; we have turned every one to his own way; and the Lord hath laid on Him the iniquity of us all.*

Isaiah 53:5-6

There are two schools. One says He's a Messiah King. The other says He's Messiah, the suffering Savior. Jesus stepped up in the middle of them and said, "Fools! Understand all that the prophets have said!" It never occurred to them that He might be Messiah Ben-Yosef and Messiah Ben-judah simultaneously.

The same thing is happening today. "God will supply all your needs," some tell us.[13] "Anything you need will be done. You don't have to worry. It's already there for you. You won't suffer. God will prosper you, make you rich, and supply anything you need.[14] Do you believe that? Do you want it? If you serve God, you will live in a big house and drive a new car. God will give you a better job. Everything will be wonderful because He is the supplier of every need." To some, He is Messiah Ben-Judah.

Others say that if you do drive a new car and live in a big house, you're going to hell.[15] To them, He is Messiah Ben-Yosef, the suffering Savior. They say we need to pray harder, that "we must seek God."

We still have the same fight. Fools! It never dawned on us that there is a wholeness in the gospel that teaches us that "all that will live godly in Christ Jesus shall suffer persecution."[16] The same Christ who allows you to suffer also raises you up in glory.[17]

"I have been young, and now am old; yet have I not seen the righteous forsaken, nor his seed begging bread" (Ps. 37:25).

It is confusing to me that those two men on the road to Emmaus didn't know Jesus for seven-and-one-half miles. How can two men go seven-and-one-half miles with their best Friend,[18] Teacher,[19] Preacher,[20] and Bishop,[21] and not know Him? Then He can sit down at a table and break some bread, and they say, "Oh, it's Jesus." What did He do at the table that He couldn't do in seven-and-one-half miles? He did something at that table that caused their eyes to open, and they knew Him. They knew something had happened because their hearts had burned within them as He taught them the Scriptures. They didn't know what was happening. That's faith. You know something is happening, but you don't know what it is.[22] We should look more carefully at what He did at that table if it was so powerful that it made them recognize Him.

> *And it came to pass, as He sat at meat with them, He took bread, and blessed it, and brake, and gave to them.*
>
> *And their eyes were opened, and they knew Him; and He vanished out of their sight.*
>
> Luke 24:30-31

He took it, He blessed it, He broke it, and gave it. "Poof!" Their eyes were opened.

1. He took bread.

2. He blessed it.

3. He broke it.

4. He gave it.

This was not a haphazard table-side manner. It is an order in the Spirit. It was so powerful that it has to be a key. You can beat against the gates of hell all day long and come back bruised and battered. Those gates may be bent a little, but you're in trouble. He didn't say He'd give you power to knock down the gates of hell. He said the gates of hell shall not prevail against you because you have the keys to the Kingdom.

> *And I say also unto thee, That thou art Peter, and upon this rock I will build My church; and the gates of hell shall not prevail against it.*

And I will give unto thee the keys of the kingdom of heaven: and whatsoever thou shalt bind on earth shall be bound in heaven: and whatsoever thou shalt loose on earth shall be loosed in heaven.

Matthew 16:18-19

If you ever get the keys, you can just unlock the gate.[23] You don't have to wrestle with it.

This is a key: He took it. He blessed it. He broke it. He gave it. Their eyes were opened. How do we know that's not a haphazard thing?

And He said unto them, With desire I have desired to eat this passover with you before I suffer:

For I say unto you, I will not any more eat thereof, until it be fulfilled in the kingdom of God.

And He took the cup, and gave thanks, and said, Take this, and divide it among yourselves:

For I say unto you, I will not drink of the fruit of the vine, until the kingdom of God shall come.

And He took bread, and gave thanks, and brake it, and gave unto them, saying, This is My body which is given for you: this do in remembrance of Me.

Luke 22:15-19

He did the same thing!

And when it was evening, His disciples came to Him, saying, This is a desert place, and the time is now past; send the multitude away, that they may go into the villages, and buy themselves victuals.

But Jesus said unto them, They need not depart; give ye them to eat.

And they say unto Him, We have here but five loaves, and two fishes.

He said, Bring them hither to Me.

And He commanded the multitude to sit down on the grass, and took the five loaves, and the two fishes, and looking up to heaven, He blessed, and brake, and gave the loaves to His disciples, and the disciples to the multitude.

Matthew 14:15-19

He took the five loaves and two fishes. He blessed them. He broke them. He gave them to His disciples. It's the same thing! Do you see what I see? He didn't just do it one time. He did it the same way every time. He did it this way because there was power in doing it this way.

By this simple thing that He did every time He had bread, He explained His whole purpose in being here.[24] He was not here just to bless. He was here to be taken, to break and be broken, and to be given, also.

We cannot take one piece of what He did or one thing that He taught and cling to it as the gospel.[25] We cannot take the faith message and hang on to it until Jesus comes. We cannot accept intercessory prayer and say that is the whole gospel. We cannot take praise and worship and say that is the major part of the gospel. All these things are parts of the pie, but Jesus would say, "O fools, and slow of heart to believe all that the prophets have spoken." Christ had to suffer and then enter into His glory.

At that table, He manifested everything He had said in seven-and-one-half miles.

Moses

"And beginning at Moses..." (Lk. 24:27).

Moses' name means "drawn forth" or "taken out of." He was taken out of the river. God took him.[26]

He became the son of Pharaoh's daughter, second only to Pharaoh.[27] His education made him knowledgeable in all the arts and sciences.[28] He understood the stars and mathematics. He knew everything that could be taught by men. He rode in the king's chariot and on the king's horses. God blessed him.

Moses saw one of his kinsmen beaten by an Egyptian.[29] He killed the Egyptian and buried him in the sand. He was happy that he could help his relative; then suddenly, he had to run for his life.[30] After that, he spent 40 years on the backside of the desert helping the ladies water the sheep.[31] He went from the king's house to menial labor on the backside of the desert. God broke him.

We don't understand the process. We are happy that God took us out of darkness and brought us into marvelous light.[32] We are happy that God blessed us. When God tries to break us, we feel like He deserted us, not understanding it is part of the process.[33]

We have churches full of people who can walk with Him, talk to Him, and listen to His message, but they don't know Him. They never go through the order. They come short of the purpose of God. They say, "God, take me. God, bless me. God, bless me. God, bless me. God, bless me." When it comes to being broken, they say, "Unh-unh! That's not what I heard on the tape!"

Moses tended sheep for 40 years in Midian. At the end of that time, he marched into Pharaoh's court, and said, "Let My people go!"[34] God gave him to the people as a deliverer and a savior.

God will not give you until He has had the opportunity to break you. If you do not want the breaking, you don't need the glory. If you don't go through the pain, you don't need the power.[35] You would pervert it.[36]

David

"He chose David also His servant, and took him from the sheepfolds: from following the ewes great with young He brought him to feed Jacob His people, and Israel His inheritance" (Ps. 78:70-71).

David was just a shepherd boy following the mother sheep around when Eliab came and took him to Samuel the seer, after the prophet had rejected Eliab. David was the youngest of his brothers, but God took him.

He was killing giants when he was only a boy.[37] The maidens sang songs exalting him above the king.[38] He sat at the king's table.[39] God blessed him.

He had to run for his life from Saul for 15 years.[40] He had a city and someone burned it down.[41] He had wives and men stole them.[42] Six hundred of his own men wanted to stone him.[43] God broke him.

God gave him Judah and Israel.[44] God gave him a Messiah for a son.[45] God gave him. That's the order of breaking bread.

Joseph

God took Joseph miraculously from the barren womb of Rachel.[46]

Joseph saw visions. The sun, the moon, and the stars bowed down before him.[47] Because his father favored Joseph above his brothers, he put a coat on him that he had never placed on his brothers.[48] He was blessed.

His brothers sold him into slavery.[49] He worked as a slave in Potiphar's house.[50] A dungeon became his home.[51] He was broken.

God raised him up. He cast corn on the water to save nations of people, including his entire family, from starvation.[52] God gave Joseph to his people.

Every man ever used of God went through an order that gave them the power to greatness. They didn't become what they were by passing over other things.

People don't want the process. They want the glory. Don't give me crosses—give me crowns. Don't give me suffering—give me healing and feeling. Don't give me lonely prayer—give me praise and worship. "O fools, and slow of heart to believe all...."

People in the "faith camp" are always telling you what God will do. They don't understand that God blessed you and now He's breaking you in order to use you. That order continues even after He has given you. God starts over. He wants to take you a little higher. He takes you. He blesses you. He breaks you. He gives you. Then He takes you higher.[53]

He was made known unto them in the breaking of bread.

Endnotes—Chapter 5

1. John 14:9
2. Genesis 3:15
3 Matthew 15:14; Luke 6:39; John 9:41; Revelation 3:17-18
4. Matthew 23:25
5. Matthew 23:27
6. Revelation 19:11
7. Revelation 19:15
8. Luke 1:32
9. Psalm 22:28; 2 Timothy 4:18; Psalm 103:19
10. Genesis 37:24
11. Genesis 39:20
12. Genesis 39:1
13. Philippians 4:19
14. 3 John 2
15. 2 Timothy 6:9-10; Colossians 3:2; Matthew 6:19-21
16. 2 Timothy 3:12
17. 2 Timothy 2:12; Romans 6:5
18. John 15:13
19. John 3:2
20. Mark 2:2
21. 1 Peter 2:25
22. Hebrews 11:1
23. Revelation 1:18
24. Luke 24:26; Acts 17:3

25. Matthew 4:4
26. Exodus 2:9-10
27. Hebrews 11:26
28. Acts 7:22
29. Exodus 2:11
30. Exodus 2:15
31. Exodus 2:17
32. 1 Peter 2:9
33. Job 2:9
34. Exodus 5:1
35. Hebrews 12:8
36. Luke 7:30
37. 1 Samuel 17:46,51
38. 1 Samuel 18:7-8
39. 1 Samuel 20:5
40. 1 Samuel 23:25-26
41. 1 Samuel 30:1
42. 1 Samuel 30:5; 2 Samuel 3:14-16
43. 2 Samuel 15:14
44. 2 Samuel 5:5
45. Mark 12:35-37
46. Genesis 30:22-24
47. Genesis 37:9
48. Genesis 37:3
49. Genesis 37:28
50. Genesis 39:1

51. Genesis 39:20
52. Genesis 41:57
53. 2 Corinthians 3:18

Chapter 6

The Finished Work
Suffering Successfully

We need to receive some things from God with joy.[1] We can receive blessings with joy easily, but other things are difficult to receive.

For I am in a strait betwixt two, having a desire to depart, and to be with Christ; which is far better:

Nevertheless to abide in the flesh is more needful for you.

And having this confidence, I know that I shall abide and continue with you all for your furtherance and joy of faith;

That your rejoicing may be more abundant in Jesus Christ for me by my coming to you again.

Only let your conversation be as it becometh the gospel of Christ: that whether I come and see you, or else be absent, I may hear of your affairs, that ye stand fast in one spirit, with one mind striving together for the faith of the gospel;

And in nothing terrified by your adversaries: which is to them an evident token of perdition, but to you of salvation, and that of God.

For unto you it is given in the behalf of Christ, not only to believe on Him, but also to suffer for His sake;

Having the same conflict which ye saw in me, and now hear to be in me.

Philippians 1:23-30

"So that my bonds in Christ are manifest in all the palace, and in all other places" (Phil. 1:13).

There are very distinct phases of worship. One is supplication, simple thanksgiving centered in what we offer to God.[2] We thank the Lord for what He does and what He is. Supplication is a very private and personal feeling. We lift ourselves to God. "Oh, Jesus, I want You to take me. I love You. I reach toward You. I thank You for light. I thank You for Your presence." Simple thanksgiving is lifting ourselves to God. We sup with Him, and He sups with us. We eat with Him, and He eats with us. Supplication is the gentle knocking at the door, the gentle touch of God that causes us to look upward.

"Behold, I stand at the door, and knock: if any man hear My voice, and open the door, I will come in to him, and will sup with him, and he with Me" (Rev. 3:20).

The next phase of worship is praise. We shout with a loud voice.[3] At the end of every song, we say things like, "Oh, hallelujah, thank You, Jesus. You are great, Lord. We give You glory. Praise God. Oh, glory to God. He is great and greatly to be praised."[4]

Sometimes our praise falls short because it becomes habitual. Our praise language is usually about six months old. We say the things we learn in the first five or six months of our Christian experience. We echo them for the rest of our lives.

We should use the Word of God in prayer and praise. The Word of God is spiritual inspiration.[5] We should memorize some Psalms and other precious Scriptures in the New Testament. They are living words.[6] If we quote them while we praise, it opens the door to new inspiration.

Using the Word of God in praise is like throwing a stick of dynamite against a hill. It blows open a big cave. Now you can go wander around through deep, new places where, beforehand, you were only scratching in the sand. We need the Word of God to blow the door open to make our praise more fluent.

The third phase of worship, rejoicing in the Lord, is the one in which we have lacked proficiency.

1. Thanksgiving, or personal supplication. The first is what we feel He is to us, and what we are to Him.

2. Praise, giving laud and praise about what He is. The second is what He is to us.

3. Rejoicing. The third phase encompasses everything from dancing to laughing in the Holy Ghost. There is a holy laughter.

Uncle Lester

I went to one of our first revival meetings in the hills of West Virginia at my Uncle Lester's church. He was one of the slowest people I ever knew. I am not saying he lacked intelligence. He was just slow. He walked slow, talked slow, and went slow. He was 35 before he married. He even got married slow. He married my daddy's sister, and she was slow. She was 33 when she got married.

I will never forget when Uncle Lester became fast. He was pastoring 18 or 19 people. We started having revival and filled up the building with 150 people. People were looking in the windows because there was not enough room for them to come in.

A funeral caused that revival. Sometimes funerals cause good things to happen. All these people decided it was time to go to church. We were baptizing people, and they were receiving the Holy Ghost.

Uncle Lester was sitting on a chair, rocking back and forth, so happy for the people who were coming to God. More people received the Holy Ghost in just a few nights than he had seen in years. He said, "Thank You, Jesus. Thank You, Jesus." Then he stopped, and said, "I wish I could find a bigger praise than this."

A holy laughter hit him as soon as he said that. He fell off his chair to the floor. "Ha! Ha! Ha! Ha! Ha! Ha! Whew! Hoo! Hoo! Hoo! Heee! Heee! Ha! Ha! Ha!"

He laughed until he scared me to death. I thought he had lost his mind. He did more than just giggle a little. He laid down and held his stomach. He rocked back and forth, rolling from elbow to elbow. He would sit back up and lie back down. Some people might think it was stupid, but he moved into a realm of worship that went beyond saying words to God. It went into his spirit and became a part of his physical structure.

Dancing before the Lord is like that. It is more than an emotional takeover you cannot control. Our past exuberance is spiritual frustration, the helicopter mode. Kicking and falling over the benches is not necessary. You can rejoice in the Lord by praising Him out of your spirit and manifesting it through your body. It is a very beautiful thing.

The Bible said we worship Him with our bodies.[7] Worship goes beyond clapping and lifting hands. There should be a manifestation of worship that takes over the mental and spiritual processes until you no longer care what people think or who is looking.

When you receive the baptism of the Holy Ghost, you will hug the person closest to you regardless of who is in the house. The Holy Ghost overcomes all inhibition. But a few days later, your experience wears down and you become reasonable again. When we receive the baptism of the Holy Ghost, we receive a foretaste of our inheritance, not just in Heaven, but in the Church. His inheritance is in the Church.

In the first chapter of the Book of Ephesians, Paul said there were three things he was praying about for the Ephesian church:

1. He wanted them to know what was the hope of the calling of the Lord.[8]

2. He wanted them to know the riches of the glory of His inheritance in the saints (not in Heaven, but the glorious inheritance in the Church).[9]

3. He wanted them to know what is the exceeding greatness of His power to us who believe.[10]

The love of God is shed abroad in our hearts by the Holy Ghost.[11] The love of God works. It is impossible for the love of God to work in our hearts unless we have more than two phases of worship.

What does the Bible say we have in the Holy Ghost?

1. We have righteousness. Righteousness gives us supplication and thanksgiving, the little praise that comes up out of our hearts and says, "Cleanse me, O God. I give You glory because I know Your blood can cover me right now."

2. We have peace. When we give God glory, the peace of God floods our hearts.

3. Joy, or rejoicing.

Righteousness, peace, and joy in the Holy Ghost.[12]

Righteousness is the level of worship that gives us supplication and thanksgiving. Righteousness was what God wanted them to know was the hope of the calling of the Lord. Thanksgiving, or personal supplication, is what we feel He is to us, and what we are to Him. He is made unto us righteousness.[13] We are unto Him the righteousness of God in Christ Jesus.

When we give God glory, the peace of God floods our hearts.[14] He wanted them to know the riches of the glory of His inheritance in the saints, not in Heaven, but the glorious inheritance in the Church.

Rejoicing is what God wanted them to know. Rejoicing is the exceeding greatness of His power to us who believe. Rejoicing, the third phase, encompasses everything from dancing to laughing in the Holy Ghost. Rejoicing is what gives us power. The joy of the Lord is our strength.[15]

There should be personal supplication. There should be glory given to God. There should be rejoicing in the Lord. Rejoicing in the Lord goes beyond saying words to Him. There is a real joy, a happiness, a feeling that surmounts and overcomes our sorrows and problems.

The Scripture teaches us to rejoice in tribulation,[16] temptation,[17] and fiery trials.[18] We are to rejoice that we are partakers of His suffering.[19] We must learn how to suffer successfully. Until we do, we can only master two areas of worship.

Righteousness comes through repentance,[20] the shed blood,[21] and the process of the new birth.[22] You may be able to do the work of God because you have to. You give God praise because you have to. Your normal worship is always in the first phase. "O God, I love You, Jesus. Here I am, O God. Cleanse us tonight, O God. Hallelujah! Thank You, Jesus." It is in the supplication phase.

When we enter into shouting,[23] praising God, clapping hands,[24] or exuberant praise that gives laud to His name, we lose a whole group of people. Some people only have enough worship to keep righteousness. They serve God because they don't want to go to hell. They witness because they know if they don't witness and share their experience, they become the Dead Sea. Their experience in God is a "must" situation, so their worship will never climb beyond the simple righteousness stage. They never can enter into praise, exalted glory, and rejoicing. We lose a whole group of people who cannot go beyond a personal expression to God and a personal feeling of getting right. Their prayers start with, "O God, I know I've failed You again this week, but You know my heart, O God. I want to live for You." They have never been able to know the mercy of God, to trust the blood of Jesus and the grace of God that is greater than all their failings, and enter into a phase where they can say, "God, You are great and greatly to be praised.[25] Hallelujah! As the mountains are round about Jerusalem, so the Lord is round about His people."

Praise is not as personal as it is general in the Church. Praise becomes more than personal feeling. It rises until it becomes part of the general congregation. "I will praise the Lord in the congregation." It is not the praise you offer from yourself, but it overflows into someone else. You can share it. It becomes horizontal. You can gather up a glorious praise from the Church. We can praise Him and thank Him because we know we must suffer and endure tribulation, so we will. We say, "It's the will of God, so I'll do it." We have peace about it. "They that live godly in Christ Jesus shall suffer persecution. I have peace about suffering. I settled it long ago. I will live for God. It's tough, but I'll do it. I will not worry or fret about it."

To most people, this Christian experience is an excruciating experience when they have to share it. If we climb up one rung farther, we learn to become numb to suffering. We will live for God regardless of what they say.

The apostles and the early Church attained a place that, when they were beaten and persecuted,[26] they counted it joy[27] that they were able to be partakers of His suffering.[28] To them, it wasn't, "I can't stand it, but I must do it, or I'll be lost," or "I know I have to do this because that's the way it is if you live a Christian life." It was, "Come on. Hit me one more time, because that's what Jesus took. I want a little more of what He had. I want a little more of that suffering. I want to understand godly joy."

"And no man taketh this honour unto himself" (Heb. 5:4).

Nobody calls himself to work for God. There must be a recognized call of God. We have a great possibility to come to a pure, honest, and absolute authority in the ministry, and a glorious, godly, and holy response in the congregation.

If we restore the apostolic Church—and we must—we must come to a place where God can speak and minister to us. We could stop the murmuring and bickering that has always destroyed the work of God. We could come to the honest place of accepting and giving where God has always wanted His Church to be. That is the deep river that we have never been able to dredge, the one channel we have never been able to put our barges in. It is a channel of complete trust and honest living between the ministry and the congregation where you can believe that God is working. You can know that God is serving us and working with us, and that we are giving our best. That brings peace and great grace to the Church. It removes distraction and destroys confusion.

We need to learn that the things the Church considers suffering are usually nothing more than temporary tribulations trying us out to see if we can last. The things that come against us are not just to see if we received the Holy Ghost or if we are living a counterfeit life.

"for every high priest taken from among men is ordained for men" (Heb. 5:1).

He must have "compassion on the ignorant, and on them that are out of the way; for that he himself also is compassed with infirmity. And by reason hereof he ought, as for the people, so also for himself, to offer for sins" (Heb. 5:2-3).

Nobody is separated for himself. When God separates somebody to do a work, he's separated for other men. A man cannot be a part of the priesthood unless he has infirmity all around him. He has learned to endure infirmity, suffering, and sorrow with a proper, successful spirit. We cannot reconcile men to God in Christ's stead[29] unless we are willing to be partakers of His suffering. It was that agony that brought us redemption.[30]

Moses was an example of the successful spirit. Moses continued to walk with God and lead the people. Here is a man who continued steadfastly until he heard the voice of God. Moses persevered until he saw the fiery finger of God chisel out in granite stone the way for men to live.[31] Here is a man who continued until he passed on that glorious anointing to Joshua.[32] Joshua then marched across the river to take the cities of Canaan, successfully passing on what Moses had given him from God.

Korah, as a prince among the people, led 200 princes.[33] This man should have been one of the stalwart leaders they could look up to, but he suffered unsuccessfully. He was having trouble with the food, the path, and the journey like everyone else. As one of the princes of the people,[34] his load was as heavy as Moses' and everyone else's. As one of the leaders, he knew the great weight and responsibility of leadership.

Korah might have been a Joshua. He was a prince of the people and a great leader, but when it was time for strength, and suffering came upon him, he began to murmur. He joined all the other princes of the people—200 of them. They began to murmur against Moses, and said, "You led us out into this wilderness to let us die."[35]

God is always building success into people. The Kingdom of God is not a slouchy type of spirituality that lacks motivation. God's gospel is always making the best person out of us.[36] Even if you talk about success and motivation and take all the success courses, you can never do anything finer than learn to live a godly, Christian life. Christianity is the finest motivation in the whole world.

Korah was unsuccessful in his suffering. What made him go to Moses was the fact that he was having problems. He was suffering. The pressure was on him as it was on them all. When Korah came out against Moses, he leveled his complaint at the man of God. He said, "You brought us out here to let us die. You took us away from food and brought us out here to this wilderness."

God spoke to Moses and said, "Get back out of the way." The earth opened and swallowed all those murmuring people.[37]

The pressure on us is on other people too. We sometimes think we are the only people suffering. If God ever uses us for His glory, if we ever become spiritual lineage used of God, we must learn to suffer successfully. We do not have to prove we have the Holy Ghost. That is not why we suffer. There is another reason. If we do not endure these things, we will not know how to take care of and help those who are having trouble.

Some things are not obtained by listening to a preacher, praying on your knees, or worshiping God in the song service. We need some things to take us into the deeper things of God that can only be obtained suffering successfully. Successful suffering involves skill. You can say, "I'm going through it because God put it on me," and enter phase one. You can say, "I'm going through it because I know I must endure to be saved," and enter phase two. You just level out and say, "I have peace about it. That's it."

But if you go through it, like the apostle in the New Testament says we should walk through it,[38] then we gain spiritual understanding. Understanding is worship. Nothing is so much glory to God as understanding why your suffering is to the glory of God. Then you say, "I thank God this thing came, because in a few days, I will face somebody who feels just like I feel right now who does not have strength or courage, and does not know where to turn. If God didn't lay this thing on me, I wouldn't know how to help them. I wouldn't be a worthy high priest, and God couldn't separate me unless He could impart suffering to me."

"Ye are partakers of Christ's suffering" (1 Pet. 1:7).

We say we want to be like Jesus.[39] There are some things about Jesus we do not want to be like. What about nails and thorns?[40]

"He is despised and rejected of men; a man of sorrows, and acquainted with grief: and we hid as it were our faces from Him..." (Is. 53:3).

We hate for people to turn us down. Nothing hurts your pride more than somebody saying "No" to you when you want to help them or keep company with them so much. Rejection is terrible for a child. Rejection is one of the most terrible things in life. Christianity holds some harrowing, haunting feelings for some people because they cannot stand the possibility that they will be separated from somebody. The first thing that separates men from God is the unwillingness to be separated unto God. If we ever walk with God, we must be separated unto the gospel.

"Wherefore come out from among them, and be ye separate, saith the Lord...and [I] will be a Father unto you, and ye shall be My sons and daughters, saith the Lord Almighty" (2 Cor. 6:17-18).

People don't like physical disciplines in the Church. They don't like standards to live by. They don't want the preacher telling them what to do, where to go, or how to look. Some people go so far in the gospel and then rebel because they can't stand the possibility of rejection. They have never climbed to the lofty peaks to understand that something is imparted to a congregation that is willing to forego the works of the flesh[41] and its manifestation, and put away the things that make it worldly, selfish, and showy.[42] God's people were never meant to be so much like the world that you couldn't tell them apart. Something always separated the spirits, minds, attitudes, and physical appearance of people in the Church from those in the world. The Church of Jesus Christ is not like everybody else.

Physical disciplines are not shameful things we have to accept as something we must do. They are a part of a glorious revelation that brings a glorious joy when you suddenly say, "I am so glad I have the opportunity to line up with whatever it was that nailed Him on a cross, backed Him up, and put stripes on His back." If somebody walks by and makes fun of me, I am glad to be a part of whatever it is that separates me unto God.[43] Even if it's more than is necessary to be saved, my goal is not to do the least I can to please Him, but to do everything I can to please Him.[44] I am not working on minimums, but on maximums. I am not working on minors, but on majors.[45] I want to be more than saved. I want to be a minister of the gospel. I want God to use me.

I need more than joy. I want to learn joy through suffering. I don't obtain joy just because I'm standing here with my mouth on the floor and God comes and lifts me up. That's what we think rejoicing is. We say, "Oh God, I'm in terrible shape. Please, Jesus, come and help me. Thank God. Help me through it, Jesus." You say, "Whew! I feel the presence of the

Lord. I feel so much better." We pray ourselves right out of all these victories. We ask the preacher to lay hands on us and deliver us out of all these great possibilities.

We are so anxious to go beyond suffering that we don't realize we click ourselves back down to the second phase and go into a holding pattern, never able to move into an apostolic phase of worship that is more than saying, "I love You, Jesus. I praise You, Jesus." If we could reach out into the third phase and stay there, we could put both feet and hands out with a back beaten and be singing songs to God at midnight.[46] That's what shakes jail houses. We missed that power because we never learned to suffer successfully. How can we expect to raise the dead and cause people to get up out of wheelchairs and walk if we can't stand a headache without taking an aspirin?[47]

Stop in the middle of phase two to say, "This is not just physical affliction. I don't belong to myself. I belong to God. I don't live for myself. I live for God. I'm not my own. I belong to Him. Since I'm His child, He cares more about me than I care for myself, and there's more in this for me than I know anything about, so I will trust Him. I will start rejoicing because I know He's working out something for my good, although I don't know what it is right now. I'll begin to praise Him for it right now while I don't understand it." Now you're getting close, almost at the door. Now you can start saying, "Oh thank You, Jesus. Hallelujah! Thank You, Jesus."

I'm not talking about putting on a show. Let it come out of your spirit with understanding. "I wouldn't be suffering this if the Lord weren't putting something in me to make me useful in the Kingdom of God. This must be something I will face in the next convert I meet. What I am suffering must be something she or he is suffering."

So also Christ glorified not Himself to be made an high priest; but He that said unto Him, Thou art My Son....

As He saith also in another place, Thou art a priest for ever after the order of Melchisedec.

Hebrews 5:5-6

Since Jesus was the Son of God and perfect in His flesh, then He wouldn't have to do any praying or crying, would He?

Who in the days of His flesh, when He had offered up prayers and supplications with strong crying and tears unto Him that was able to save Him from death, and was heard in that He feared.

Hebrews 5:7

Jesus knew who He was talking to. He was still connected to the Father.[48] He was still doing the will of God.[49] Jesus had the birthright.[50]

That's another phase of impartation. An old patriarch laid his hands on that son, and he became the head of the house. Even when Jacob crossed his hands, Manasseh received it and Ephraim was left out. Joseph said, "Hey, you have your hand on the wrong one." Jacob said, "No, I did it on purpose." The head the right hand touched was the one who received it.[51] Impartation was strong, even through the patriarch.

Jesus already had the relationship down. His family relationship had already settled His priesthood. He was called the Son of God.[52] He was the Son of the Father. He was the Son of a priest.

Even though He was called, the hand of God was on Him. He would be the One who would do it, "...yet learned He obedience by the things which He suffered."[53]

Endnotes—Chapter 6

1. Isaiah 12:3
2. Philippians 4:6
3. Psalm 132:16
4. Psalm 48:1; 96:4
5. 2 Peter 1:21
6. John 6:63
7. Mark 12:30
8. Ephesians 1:18
9. Ephesians 1:18
10. Ephesians 1:19
11. Romans 5:5
12. Romans 14:17
13. 1 Corinthians 1:30
14. Philippians 4:7
15. Nehemiah 8:10
16. Romans 5:3
17. James 1:2
18. 1 Peter 4:12-13
19. 1 Peter 4:13
20. Romans 2:4
21. Matthew 26:28
22. John 3:3,5
23. Psalm 5:11; 32:11; 35:27

24. Psalm 47:1
25. Psalm 48:1; 96:4
26. Acts 16:25; 5:40
27. James 1:2
28. 1 Peter 4:13
29. 2 Corinthians 5:20
30. Luke 23:32-49
31. Exodus 31:18; Deuteronomy 9:10
32. Numbers 27:18-23
33. Numbers 16:1-2
34. Numbers 16:1
35. Numbers 16:13
36. Philippians 3:14
37. Numbers 16:21
38. Matthew 5:10-12; Acts 5:41
39. Romans 8:29
40. Philippians 3:10
41. Galatians 5:19-21
42. Colossians 3:8
43. Matthew 5:44
44. Colossians 1:10; 1 John 3:22
45. Philippians 3:13
46. Acts 16:25
47. Exodus 15:26; Psalm 103:3

48. John 17:21
49. Luke 22:42
50. Genesis 25:31-34
51. Genesis 48:13-19
52. Matthew 3:17; 17:5
53. Hebrews 5:8

Chapter 7

The Finished Work From the Oil to the Gold

When they poured the sticky oil on David's head, he never would have dreamed it would be 15 years from the oil to the gold. From the time that old man of God stood with trembling hand and poured that horn of oil on his head,[1] it would be 15 years before they would set him on a throne.[2] He would be chased like a rabbit through the briar patch. He would be down in Philistia acting like a madman, trying to keep himself away from the Philistines.[3] He would be incorporated into the army of Philistia to fight against the people of God.[4] He would be hiding in caves,[5] running for his life, and meeting Jonathan on the sly.[6]

What was wrong with this guy? He was learning to wear a crown and to be used of God. What if he had suffered unsuccessfully in those 15 years? What if he had stopped after about 10 years, and said, "My God, there's no way I can go on like this. If this is what it takes to be a king, I don't want to be a king. I can raise my family in Ziklag. I don't have to go through all this. We don't have to live like this. I'll get these men to be my bodyguards. They'll be loyal to me. I don't have to go up there and fight for the throne of a madman who throws fits every night, throws javelins at singers, and goes into temper tantrums. I will not live this way. I'll go out here and get myself a life. I'll build myself a little kingdom. I'll do this thing by myself."

When the will of God came to him, it was also the will of God for him to suffer. After they slipped the crown on his head, one of the first things he did was ask, "Where's Mephibosheth, that little crippled boy of Jonathan's?[7] I used to hate weakness. I can't stand men who won't stand the fight, but I want to set that boy at my table. Every time I walk in here to eat, I want to see his crippled, twisted limbs." What did that to this big, barrel-chested, ruddy man who came out of the shepherd's field with oil in his hair? In that 15 years of suffering and agony, something was imparted to him through running and leaving dusty trails that he could never have obtained by going to school. That caused him to pick up a crippled boy and sit him down at his table every time he came to dinner.

Nothing hurts me more than the jokes and laughter made about people who are weak in understanding. Preachers often make the dumb things people do their target of jest. God's ministry and priesthood should be elevated. Some men just don't understand. To them, people are just tithe payers and saints are just churchgoers. They just get what they can out of saints and other ministers, and coexist until the Lord comes. That is not what God intended His work to be. His work is a maturing place, where we can "grow up in Him, which is the head even Christ, until we came to the full measure of the stature of Christ." We can become useful in the Kingdom of God. Everyone can fulfill a calling and ministry worthy of His gospel and suffering.

"Called of God an high priest after the order of Melchisedec" (Heb. 5:10).

The writer of the Book of Hebrews launches into something felt by many pastors and people who dared to fast, pray, and seek after God. He said, "You've heard about this many times. I see you are exhausted, tired, and dull of hearing, but you should be teachers of these things, and you need someone to teach you again the first principles of the oracles."[8] The laying on of hands is one of the first principles.[9] He called them "babes needing milk" rather than "men eating meat."[10] "You must get beyond basic things. We must go on.[11] To do the work of God, we must launch out into the Spirit. You cannot learn joy and rejoicing."

Rejoicing is not a superficial thing you put on your face when you walk into church. The joy of the Lord is not something you come in and say. Joy is a big, deep thing down in your soul that has learned to recognize that God is allowing suffering. Suffering is not "God being mean" or putting something bad on you. God is allowing this thing to happen in your life. He pulled up the fence[12] and let the boils come,[13] the wind blow,[14] and the fire sweep.[15] Whatever it is in my life, from a headache to a housebreak, from a car wreck to a funeral, GOD Almighty knows what must be in me before I can be able to succor those who are tempted.[16]

We need to be successful in our suffering. When fiery trials come, the preacher says, "Count it all joy!"[17] He didn't say, "Just stand back and hold on. One of these days you'll understand." That's phase two. Apostles always stood in the maximum position. They went to third gear. They laid it all the way back, hit the pedal to the floor, and said, "Count it all joy when you fall into diverse temptations."

What did he say about that fiery trial? "Think it not strange."[18] Don't say, "Oh, dear, I don't know if I've lost God. I don't know if God will hear me. I don't know if I can feel anything anymore. I may not be saved." Don't talk like that. The apostle has already made it clear to us that we should line up what we say with the Word of God.[19]

"Only let your conversation be as it becometh the gospel of Christ..." (Phil. 1:27).

Don't get into a trial and start talking like the flesh. Don't get into a trial and say, "I don't know why these things happen. You would think God would look out after us. We paid our tithes for the last five years." Don't talk like that. Stop and think. God knows you better than you know yourself.[20] He knows what you need better than you do. Open your mouth in praise to God. If you can ever arrive to that place where you can successfully suffer, and say, "I don't understand it, but I know God does. I am so thankful that He has enough confidence in my strength that He can lay this burden on me. I will carry it through the cloud to the victory because it will make me stronger. It will make me love God. It will make me a soul winner. It will make me successful. Hallelujah!

"God knows that next thing that will happen to me down the road. If I don't get phase two, I will not be able to take phase three. If I can't live through this one, I'll never make it through that one. I must stand in this thing."

"...be strong in the Lord, and in the power of His might. Put on the whole armour of God, that ye may be able to stand..." (Eph. 6:10-11).

Another place in worship is imparted through suffering. It takes a catastrophe for us to realize how much we have to be thankful for.

"For unto you it is given in the behalf of Christ, not only to believe on Him, but also to suffer for His sake" (Phil. 1:29).

God did not call you just to believe in Him and trust in His gospel, but also to suffer for His sake. Over 100 Scriptures in the New Testament refer to suffering for Him.

"Wherefore Jesus also, that He might sanctify the people with His own blood, suffered.... Let us go forth therefore unto Him...bearing His reproach" (Heb.13:12-13).

It is given unto us to do more than just believe on Him and obtain salvation. He wants you to be more than saved. He also wants you to learn to suffer, because it's also given to you to suffer for His sake.

Everybody in this whole world suffers. Rich and poor men suffer. Their suffering is not always of the same origin, but it is often the same in intensity. I have seen happy poor people and sad rich people, and sad poor people and happy rich people. Everybody's joy and pain does not spring from the same origin. What makes one person happy doesn't necessarily make somebody else happy. One man wants to go swimming, but another wants to go fishing. This lady wants to go shopping, but another wants to baby-sit. The sinner suffers agony and anguish, but he doesn't have any hope to hold on to.

The apostle Paul said, "If all I had was in this life, I would be of all men most miserable."[21] He was a man educated in the arts in the schools of Tarsus.[22] He understood religious orders. He had been at the feet of Gamaliel.[23] He had the best spiritual and physical training that the mind can have. He was both a Jew and a Roman citizen. He had the best of all worlds. He could walk in where the Jews went, and say, "I am a Pharisee,"[24] or where the Romans went, and they would have to say, "Don't touch him, boys. That man's a Roman citizen."[25] He could live either with the lowly Jews in captivity, or with the Romans in sovereignty. He could walk through all those worlds with his head held high. Yet he proclaimed that if all the hope he had was in this world, he would be a miserable man.

Our gasoline runs out like everybody else's. The bread supply gets low. You have to pay for air conditioning if you stay cool in the summer. Your house gets termites just like the fellow down the block who cusses and spits tobacco. It makes no difference. If you live in this life, you have problems.[26] It's not so much the suffering of Christ as it is just living life. You have trouble in this life.

There is only one difference in this between the sinner and the Christian. God, who governs life, adjusts trouble for the Christian and puts it in an order that is best for him. With the sinner, trouble comes any way it comes. It's like a windstorm.

"For they have sown the wind, and they shall reap the whirlwind..." (Hos. 8:7).

The sinner gets the storm, but God's way is a very concise, reasonable, understandable, purposeful, and direct operation. When you give your life completely and totally to Him, He takes all your joy, sadness, hopes, and dreams, and adjusts them like a big computer. You hit a button and it files everything in a proper order. He takes all those tests and puts them in order so that He can come back to you and say,

"I won't let anything come on you that you're not able to bear." He hits another button. All those joys file out over on the other side. He has it fixed so that every time a heavy sorrow comes, a blessing follows it.

For sorrow, He gives us gladness.[27] For the oil of mourning, He gives us rejoicing. For ashes, He gives us beauty. He adjusts all the things that will ever happen in our lives according to the will of God.

If you give Him your life and keep it in His hands, nothing can happen to you that God does not ordain. "If I live, I am the Lord's.[28] If I die, I am the Lord's. The Lord giveth. The Lord taketh away. Blessed be the name of the Lord."[29] Job understood the process. Sometimes too many heavy things happen to men who do not give their lives to God. Good things happen to too few. That's why they find them hanging from their beautiful, French chandeliers. That's why they live their lives behind prison bars. That's why they weep at caskets until it is too much to understand. The will of God does not fall in order in their lives.[30]

If we turn on the faucet of blessing and say, "Okay, God, you have my life arranged well," and pull this handle and say, "I want all these blessings," then our life is left with only one big lump of sorrow. In the Christian heart, there is always that sad face and that lonely inner sickness because we believe that suffering is not the will of God. We have received every blessing and we give Him praise for it, but we are not willing to successfully live through suffering.

Our lives are empty of blessings because we swallow them all up in the sorrow we never let out of our soul. When sorrows come, I say, "I thank You for it, Lord, because it will make me strong. It will make me able to help somebody else who has the same problem. It will be the stepping stone to the next thing I need that I don't have."

God allows things to happen in our lives that we cannot plan for. They come like flashes of lightning and, before we know it, we are right in the middle of a terrible problem. When we finally get through it, we have to say, "I'm thankful I'm alive," or "I thank God. If it hadn't been for God, I don't know what I would have done. I couldn't have stood it. I couldn't have made it. I wouldn't be here."[31]

We don't understand how we could ever rejoice in anything like that, but we should thank God for some tragic things that have happened in our lives. Without them, we might not be feeling the touch of God today. Sometimes we look back to them, and say, "That's the thing that brought me to God."

People come to God because their houses burn or they lose their wives, their husbands, or their children. People come to God because they take so many drugs that their habit may reach more than $200 a day. Hopeless and helpless, they finally wind up in psychiatric wards. People come to God because they are alcoholics. Families and children are saved because of what God does in the life of one alcoholic husband.

The tragedy is those people who have suffered just like the rest of us, but their suffering brought them bitterness or misunderstanding. Their suffering finally caused them to succumb to the same spirit of that temptation that they suffered successfully under for so long. Like Demas,[32] they gave up altogether and became spiritual has-beens. They said, "What's the use? Why should I go to church if God doesn't care about me? Those people don't love me. Some man talked bad to me in that church. That usher set my little boy down too hard on the seat. I don't have to live like that." Suffering would have made them stronger. Suffering could have been the gearshift into the most dynamic spiritual worship of all. You can have the most hideous tribulation and give God the most glorious worship available, rejoicing in Him. Instead, it becomes the disaster of angry spirits, hatred, bitterness, emulations, wrath, malice, and the works of the flesh until, eventually, men are drowned and overcome with heresies and seditions because they could not suffer successfully.

It started somewhere way back along the road—somewhere, somehow, somebody did somebody else wrong. Somebody said something wrong that triggered a succession of things pouring out of their souls. They forgot to count the blessings with the pain. They let it become a stumbling block. It destroyed them rather than giving them a step up into apostolic worship.

I watched a little lady dance in the Spirit in the service one night. She danced, rejoiced, and laughed in the Spirit. She would dance to the end of the aisle, clap her hands, and dance back down the aisle so gracefully. The pastor leaned over to me, and said, "That woman has won more people to God than anybody in this church." I said, "That is wonderful." I thought, "She's rejoicing because of all the souls she has won." I leaned over to the pastor, and said, "Pastor, is her family here?" He said, "Oh, no! Her husband is an alcoholic. He beats her every night when she gets home from church. Her only son is in prison for killing a man. When she came to God, she found it so joyful to serve Him that it doesn't matter about the suffering. She wins more souls than healthy men, or than women who have good husbands in the church. She doesn't ever open her mouth except to speak good and kind things about somebody."[33] He finished speaking with a statement that stirred my heart, *"That lady has learned to suffer successfully."* I never forgot what he said when he shook his finger at that woman as she danced, "She learned to suffer successfully."

She moved into a place of worship that made her a high priest because infirmity surrounded her. She was able to help the ignorant and those who are out of the way.

Endnotes—Chapter 7

1. 1 Samuel 16:13
2. 2 Samuel 2:4
3. 1 Samuel 27:1
4. 1 Samuel 28:1
5. 1 Samuel 24:3
6. 1 Samuel 23:16
7. 2 Samuel 9:1-6
8. Hebrews 5:11-12
9. Hebrews 6:1
10. Hebrews 5:13
11. Hebrews 6:1
12. Job 1:10
13. Job 2:7
14. Job 1:19
15. Job 1:16
16. Hebrews 2:18
17. James 1:2
18. 1 Peter 4:12
19. 1 Peter 3:8-13
20. Hebrews 4:13
21. 1 Corinthians 15:19
22. Acts 21:39
23. Acts 22:3
24. Acts 23:6; 26:5; Philippians 3:5
25. Acts 22:25-29

26. 1 Corinthians 10:13
27. Isaiah 61:3
28. Romans 14:8
29. Psalm 104:28-29
30. Romans 12:2
31. Psalm 119:92
32. 2 Timothy 4:10
33. Ephesians 4:29

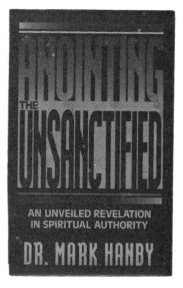

Audio Tapes Available From Dr. Mark Hanby

Anointing Series $25.00
Communion Series... $25.00
Consecration Series $25.00
Doors of Prayer Series... $35.00
Eagle, The... $18.00
Glory Series.. $25.00
Multiplicity of Ministry Series.. $35.00
Prayer and the Heavenlies... $18.00
Sovereignty of God Series.. $18.00
Suffering Series $25.00
What If God Should Get Hungry? $18.00

Available From Destiny Image
Call Toll Free:
1-800-722-6774